Joe Castello was born in 1939. He graduated in Pharmacy and now leads a family business that majors on pubs and clubs. He was active in rugby, Judo and ski-ing until common sense prevailed. He still plays in a rock 'n' roll band. He has a son who is diabetic.

THE JOE PUBLIC GUIDE TO THE SICILIAN MAFIA

Joe Castello

THE JOE PUBLIC GUIDE TO THE SICILIAN MAFIA

AUSTIN MACAULEY
PUBLISHERS LTD.

A CIP catalogue record for this title is available from the British Library.

ISBN 978 14963 508 0

www.austinmacauley.com

First Published (2014)
Austin Macauley Publishers Ltd.
25 Canada Square
Canary Wharf
London
E14 5LB

Printed and bound in Great Britain

Contents

Introduction

This book, like others in the series, sets out to reduce its subject to a summary of headlines.

This approach of producing an overview satisfies many, including those who don't derive much pleasure from the act of reading. Others however may find that their appetites have merely been whetted, and that they need much more than can be provided by this publication.

In these cases, I need to refer them to the universally critically acclaimed book by John Dickie, entitled COSA NOSTRA. This book is immaculately researched, and is seen by many as the gold standard for this subject.

It is COSA NOSTRA that I have used for most of my text, although I also took information from THE LAST GODFATHERS by John Follain, and from THE HONOURED SOCIETY by Norman Lewis.

For the last chapter only, I have used information from FIVE FAMILIES by Selwyn Raab, MAFIA PRINCESS by Antoinette Giancana and Thomas C Renner, THE MAFIA – THE FIRST 100 YEARS by William Balsamo and George Carpozi Jr., UNDER BOSS by Peter Maas, and from Wikipedia.

As with others in the Joe Public Guide series, all royalties from this publication will be donated to DIABETES UK.

Availability.

More information on THE JOE PUBLIC GUIDE series, and a facility to make purchases, can be obtained from: www.joepublicguide.com.

Cover design kindly donated by www.jameswellsgraphics.com

General Information

The Mafia is a highly organised criminal organisation that was born in Sicily in about 1860. It is still disturbingly active.

Mafia Families and blood families are distinct entities.

Just because one or more of a blood family have been initiated into the Mafia, it does not in any way implicate other members of the blood family.

Indeed, since Cosa Nostra is a secret organisation, it has a rule that its members must not tell their blood families anything about its affairs.

Much information about the organisation has come from individual Mafia pentiti (defectors).

Mafia has become a generic label for the whole world panoply of organised crime --- Chinese, Japanese, Russian, Chechen, Albanian, Turkish, and so on, even though they have little or nothing to do with the Sicilian original.

There are even other criminal organisations based in other regions of Italy, and all of them are sometimes called Mafia:

- The Sacra Corona Unita, in Puglia (the heel of the Italian boot)
- The 'Ndrangheta, in Calabria (the toe)
- The Camorra in Naples and the surrounds

None of them are as powerful or as well organised as the Sicilian Mafia, which gave birth to the American Mafia as a result of emigration.

In Sicily only Sicilians can be initiated into membership.

The American Mafia began as a purely Sicilian organisation but later became Pan Italian, and then American Italian.

The Mafia in Sicily pursues power and money by cultivating the art of killing people and getting away with it, and by organising itself in a unique way that combines the attributes of a shadow state, an illegal business, and a sworn secret society like the freemasons.

It acts like a state because:

- It aims to control territory and the people within it. Protection rackets are for the Mafia Family what taxes are for a legal government. The difference is that the Mafia tries to tax ALL economic activity, whether it's legal or illegal. Retailers and robbers alike, all pay what is known as "pizzo". The Mafia may well protect both the garage showroom and the gang of car thieves who prey on it.

- It gives itself the power of life and death over its subjects.

- It exists by infiltrating the legal state, and twisting it to its purpose. The Italian state must be criticised for failing to identify the problem and to deal with it. It was often complicit.

- Most of the income from protection rackets is ploughed back into maintaining its murder capability. It buys lawyers, judges, policemen, politicians and casual labour. It also supports Mafiosi who still end up in prison despite their best efforts at corruption.

The Mafia is a business because:

- It tries to make a profit.
- It uses its own brand of intimidation.
- It targets all sorts of markets, e.g. construction fraud, tobacco smuggling, narcotics distribution, prostitution, gambling, the unions etc.

Cosa Nostra is an exclusive secret society because:

- It is very selective who it initiates, and therefore to whom it gives the benefits of membership.

- Members must be discreet, obedient and ruthlessly violent.
- The famous code of silence is known as omerta.
- The worst of all crimes is for a Mafioso to become an informer (pentito [plural pentiti]).
- When a man is initiated into the Mafia, he becomes a "man of honour" and a "made man". At his initiation, he swears to always tell the truth to other "made men", regardless of which Family they are in. To not tell the truth can result in death, but always results in paranoia,

because of the fear of malicious gossip and its consequences.

Men of Honour enter into an entirely new lifestyle.

The code of honour is much more than a list of rules.

Becoming a "man of honour" means taking on a whole new identity, and entering a different moral universe.

The candidate will have been thoroughly tested, and have proved his capability to murder.

In the initiation ceremony, the candidate holds up a burning picture of the Madonna of the Annunciation, and swears allegiance and silence till death.

The burning of the sacred image symbolises his death as an ordinary man, and his rebirth as a "man of honour".

It also symbolises the annihilation of all traitors.

The new Mafioso swears his obedience to his capo, and must never ask "why?".

Honour accumulates through obedience.

A Mafioso who sleeps with another Mafioso's wife will face the death sentence.

He is also not allowed to earn money from pimping.

He is encouraged not to gamble, womanise, and parade his wealth.

The Boss of the Family was traditionally seen to lead a very humble and non-materialistic lifestyle.

Honour also implies that a Mafioso must put the interests of Cosa Nostra before his own blood family.

In some cases, a man may work and kill for the Family, and have members of his own family who are "made men", without he himself being initiated and receiving the benefits of a "man of honour".

A mafioso will often have to ask his capo's permission to marry, as his choice is most important for the security of Cosa Nostra.

Keeping wives "sweet", was one of the reasons for the "pimping taboo".

However loyal a wife is to her Mafioso husband, she cannot be formally initiated into the Family.

The relationship of the Catholic Church with the Mafia has been deeply criticised by many, for its tolerance and lack of condemnation of such an evil force. They are seen in fact, to have cohabited far too comfortably for far too long.

As a result of Tommaso Buscetta (mentioned later) turning pentito, it was learned that:

- The Mafia was called Cosa Nostra (our thing). It had previously been assumed that this term applied only to the American mob.
- It had a pyramidal command with soldiers at the lowest level. These soldiers would employ associates to do a good deal of the front line work, so that the organisation was further insulated from prosecution. These associates would have no idea of the Family structure, and some of them would be men who were being tested for later initiation.
- The soldiers were supervised into groups of ten or so by a capodecina (head of 10). Sometimes called caporegime.

- Each capodecina reported to an elected boss (capofamiglia) of a local gang, clan, cosca or Family.
- The boss, or capo, was flanked by an underboss (sotto capo) and by one or two consiglieri (advisers), who between them ruled over a predetermined territory.
- Three families with adjoining territories were organised into a mandamento (district).
- The head of each mandamento was a member of the Commission, Cosa Nostra's parliament, or board of management for the province of Palermo.
- In theory, above this provincial level, there was a regional body made up of Mafia bosses from the whole of Sicily. In practise, Palermo dominated the Sicilian Mafia: nearly 50% of the approximate 100 Families in Sicily had their territories in Palermo and its province.
- The boss of the Palermo Commission had a leadership role within the Sicilian Mafia as a whole, and was known as the capo di tutti capi (boss of bosses).
- At the time of Buscetta's revelations, some 5,000 men of honour were members of the Sicilian Mafia.
- Significant murders – of policemen, politicians, and other Mafiosi, had to be approved and planned at the highest level, to make sure that they were compatible with the organisation's overall strategy.
- With the aim of creating stability, The Commission also issued rulings on disputes

within Families and Mandamenti. The level of internal discipline astonished investigators.

- The Sicilian Mafia and the American Mafia, to which it had given birth, had a similar structure, but they were separate organisations. Being a member in Sicily did not make you a member in the U.S. The strong links between the two were blood and business ties rather than organisational ones.

1860 – 1876

Garibaldi
The birth of the Mafia
Leopoldo Franchetti
Sidney Sonnino

In May 1860, Giuseppe Garibaldi invaded Sicily, with the aim of uniting it with the new nation of Italy.

On June 7th, Palermo became an Italian city.

Italy found it very difficult, if not impossible, to organise and rule Sicily, in the face of virtual anarchy.

There was no apparent social order, and so the Italian government declared martial law in Sicily, and repeatedly tried the military option.

This failed and life continued to be chaotic and full of strife.

In 1876, for the first time, politicians from the island entered into a new coalition government in Rome.

We have to remember that the heritage of Sicily was very rich in legacies.

Since the Greeks invaded, almost every other Mediterranean power had invaded and occupied the island.

These events probably had a cumulative effect on the psyche of Sicilians.

Contrary to popular belief, the Mafia's origins are not ancient.

The Mafia and the new nation of Italy were born together.

The ruling classes first heard òf the Mafia in the 1860's, and assumed that it was an ancient organisation that had originated in the rural heartlands, where peasants were brutally exploited on the wheat growing estates.

In truth, the Mafia emerged in an area that is still its heartland. It was where Sicily's wealth was concentrated, among the idyllic orange and lemon groves, just outside Palermo.

The Mafia's methods were honed during a period of rapid growth of the citrus fruit industry.

There was a huge demand in the mid 1800's.

- The British Royal Navy made crews take lemons to prevent scurvy.
- Citrus fruit was used to flavour Earl Grey tea.
- New York created a great demand.

In 1860, it was calculated that Sicily's lemon groves were the most profitable agricultural land in Europe.

In 1876, citrus cultivation yielded more than 60 times the average profit per hectare than for the rest of the island.

Citrus fruit gardens required a high level of investment, because the land needed to be:

- Cleared of stones.
- Terraced.
- Provided with storehouses.

- Provided with roads.
- Surrounded by protective walls.
- Irrigated and have sluices installed.

In addition:

- It took about 8 years before the trees produced fruit.
- It took several more years to become profitable.
- Lemon trees are highly vulnerable to sabotage and vandalism.

It was the combination of vulnerability and high profits that created the perfect environment for the Mafia's protection rackets.

Although there were and are lemon groves in many coastal regions of Sicily, the Mafia was, until relatively recently, overwhelmingly a western Sicily phenomenon.

It emerged in the area immediately surrounding Palermo.

Its growth was hastened by the untrustworthiness of the Italian state, which proved to be a poor competitor.

It became apparent that protection, murder, territorial dominance, competition, and collaboration between groups, were being employed in the lemon groves of the early 1870's.

A report in 1875 by the Palermo Chief of Police, claimed a detailed knowledge of the initiation ceremony undertaken by would-be Mafiosi.

This menacing initiation may have been influenced by the Freemason movement that had only arrived in Sicily in 1820.

In 1876, Leopoldo Franchetti and Sidney Sonnino, two wealthy high minded Jewish intellectuals, visited the island to conduct a private investigation into the state of Sicilian society.

One of the men they were keen to interview was Baron Turrisi Colonna, who was an expert on the subject of criminality.

He was a most respected politician, intellectual, and landowner.

He later served twice as the mayor of Palermo.

His position was rather enigmatic in that he had focussed on the Mafia, but at the same time had been pragmatic enough to cohabit with them.

The term 'Mafia' was introduced by the Italian government.

In 1877 Franchetti and Sonnino published their own research on Sicily in a substantial two part report.

Sonnino, who went on to be PM of Italy, analysed the lives of the island's landless peasants.

Franchetti's part included an analysis of the Mafia at that time.

His report has a unique stature in that it is still considered authoritative in the 21st century.

Franchetti would ultimately influence thinking about the Mafia, more than anyone else until Giovanni Falcone, over 100 years later.

He argued that the island had become a home to "the violence industry". So much so, that violence had become a form of capital that was used as part of the service sector of the Sicilian economy.

The Mafia had its protection rackets, powerful political friends, its cellular structure, its name, its rituals, and an untrustworthy state as its competitor.

The state also used the Mafia as a conspiracy theory, to justify its occasional brutal repression of political opposition.

Having said that, 1876 marked the point when the Mafia became integral to Italy's system of government.

1876 - 1890

A parliamentary enquiry
An instrument of local government

A full scale parliamentary commission of enquiry into law and order in Sicily was set up in 1875, with the intention of publishing its findings in 1877.

This enquiry was the first one to explicitly address the Mafia issue.

There was evidence as to how much Italy's rulers knew about the Mafia problem, how much they failed to combat it, and how much they actively contributed to its development.

Evidence showed how both the left and the right of Italian politics had used the Mafia as instruments of government.

It had been said that "the Mafia in Sicily is not dangerous or invincible in itself. It is dangerous or invincible because it is an instrument of local government".

The terms of the enquiry had been broadened to such an extent that the focus on the Mafia became blurred.

It was the lack of trust in the enquiry that prompted Franchetti and Sonnino to conduct their own.

The parliamentary commission's final report was apathetically received. It was also bland and wrong. It depicted the Mafia as work-shy criminals, enemies of the state, rather than as "instruments of local government".

By 1877, Italy's politicians had most of the knowledge they needed about the Mafia in order to fight it, and all of the reasons they needed to forget what they knew.

The first stage of the process by which the Mafia entered the Italian system was complete.

Soon, governments in Rome were resigning themselves to working with Sicilian politicians who had Mafia support.

Mafiosi were gradually becoming part of the new political normality.

There was a bonus for the Mafia in left wing politics. The Left spent much more on roads, bridges, harbours, hospitals, schools, sanitation, and slum clearance etc. All of these were potential sources of income for politicians and Mafiosi alike.

Under the left, the Mafia and the politicians it dealt with began to sink their arms deep into the Roman pork barrel.

The Mafia has no real inclination for politics. It merely adapts to the circumstances by striking bargains with politicians of all colours. It just follows the money!

Thus the Mafia completed its entry into the Italian political system.

The Mafia has from the onset been highly sophisticated in the way it infiltrates the leading sectors of the Sicilian economy. It is also equally sophisticated in adopting and adapting any sources of loyalty within the Sicilian culture that it can use for its own murderous purposes.

The Mafia, in other words, is anything but backward.

1890 – 1904

The Sangiorgi Report
Don Raffaele Palizzolo
Emanuele Notarbartolo

Italy was stumbling from crisis to crisis, including its humiliating attempt at colonial glory in Ethiopia.

In 1898, the PM of Italy, General Luigi Pelloux, appointed a new Chief of Police of Palermo, with instructions to tackle the Mafia.

His name was Ermanno Sangiorgi.

One of his targets would be the Mafia politician Don Raffaele Palizzolo.

He went on to author the Sangiorgi Report. This is a most important document in the history of the Mafia, although it remained undiscovered in the state archives until recent times.

The report was completed by instalments by 1900.

It was nearly 500 pages long and contained the first picture of the Sicilian Mafia ever produced.

The information was explicit, detailed, and systematic.

There was an organisational plan of the 8 Mafia cosche (Families) ruling the suburbs and satellite villages to Palermo's north and west.

The boss and underboss were named for each cosca, together with personal details of many other rank and file members.

In all, there were details on 218 men of honour.

The report also:

- Told of the Mafia's initiation ritual and code of behaviour.
- Set out its business methods. How it infiltrated and controlled the market gardens.
- How it forged money, committed robberies, terrified and murdered witnesses.
- Explained how the Mafia had centralised funds to support families of men in prison, and to pay for lawyers. This support helped maintain the vow of silence.
- Told how the bosses of the Mafia cosche worked together to manage the associations' affairs and control territory.
- Was accurate enough to mirror almost exactly with what Tommaso Buscetta sat down to reveal to Judge Falcone, decades later.

It is nothing short of amazing that Italy had this information but totally failed to respond to it.

It could have changed history.

It could have done as much damage to the Mafia as Falcone's maxi-trial of 1987.

The Sangiorgi Report, if used correctly, could have savaged the Mafia, only a few decades after it emerged.

Ermanno Sangiorgi was a career policeman who was in his late 50's at the time of the report. He came from northern-central Italy and was, and remains, all but unknown, despite his brilliant and accurate report.

At the turn on the century, Palermo was a very wealthy and stylish capital. It boasted 80 barons, 50 dukes, and 70 princes, who mingled with the crowned heads of Europe, and the moneyed elite of the time.

This era began to decline from 1908.

Sangiorgi was determined to achieve a successful prosecution against the Mafia.

It was observed that the Mafia kills people in the same way that the state does. It does not murder, it executes.

In 1901, Sangiorgi took 89 Mafiosi to court, and despite obstructions and witnesses reneging, 32 were convicted of forming a criminal association.

For Sangiorgi, it was a victory so small that it felt like a defeat. He felt rather bitter that his efforts had yielded so little.

The superb Sangiorgi Report was consigned to the archives.

The other brief given to Sangiorgi by General Pelloux in 1898, was to investigate the prominent Don Raffaele Palizzolo.

The story began when Marquis Emanuele Notarbartolo was the Mafia's 1st eminent corpse from the social elite, when he was assassinated in 1893.

Key facts include:

- He had served 3 years as Palermo's mayor in the 1870's.
- He was an upright and honest man who was anti-corruption.
- He had been governor of The Bank of Sicily.
- The Notarbartolo case became a national media circus, and divided the nation.

- Public opinion across Italy was astonished by the exposure of the Mafia's relationships with politicians, legal officials and the police.
- It took almost 7 years to bring the case to court in Milan for the 1st Notarbartolo trial.
- His son Leopoldo was the star witness, who accused Don Raffaele Palizzolo (a member of parliament), of hiring the killers, as a form of vendetta.
- Notarbartolo was known to hate Palizzolo for his dishonesty and association with criminals.
- He had crossed swords with Palizzolo both when he was mayor of Palermo, and then when he was at the Bank of Sicily.
- Palizzolo was arrested by Sangiorgi in Palermo as a result of Leopoldo's evidence in the Milan court.
- A litany of lies and deception were exposed as part of a giant cover up of Sicily's corruption.
- The second trial was held in Bologna and lasted almost 11 months.
- The jury returned verdicts of guilty for Don Raffaele Palizzolo for causing others to murder Notarbartolo, and also for Giuseppe Fontana who actually committed the murder. Both were given 30 years.
- The result divided the nation, but was seen as a blow against the corrupting influence of the Mafia.
- Six months later the Supreme Court of Appeal in Rome, quashed the whole Bologna trial on a technicality.

- There was also a huge movement of criticism in Sicily against what they considered to be an "anti-Sicily" verdict. It had galvanised a powerful coalition of conservatives and business interests behind the "pro Sicilian" lobby. The quashing of the Bologna trial may just have been a peace offering to this group.
- The retrial began in Florence in 1903, more than a decade after the murder.
- Only Fontana and Palizzolo were in the dock, but the trial still lasted about 10 months.
- There were still very large numbers of people, including prominent witnesses, who still denied the very existence of the Mafia.
- Because of the confusion, Mafia fatigue was bound to set in.
- By a majority of 8:4, the accused were acquitted.
- Palizzolo returned home to a hero's welcome, but in forthcoming elections he was seen as a liability, and was therefore rejected from power.
- Leopoldo Notarbartolo continued his career in the navy, and rose to the rank of admiral. The legal battle had cost him a fortune, and depleted the family wealth. He eventually wrote his father's biography, and died childless in his adopted home of Florence.
- Fontana left Sicily after the trial. He took his wife and four daughters to New York, to pursue his career in extortion and murder on the Mafia's new frontier.

- It can fairly be assessed that evil triumphed over good.

1893 – 1943

The Fasci
Bernadino Verro
Cesare Mori
Benito Mussolini
The siege of Gangi

As the crow flies, Corleone is only about 35k from Palermo.

By train however it takes over 4 hours to wind through the treeless mountains and hostile landscape.

Corleone had a population of about 16,000 inhabitants, many of whom were labourers on the great grain producing estates that surrounded it. They were poor, unhealthy, ignorant, and exploited.

Corleone existed to feed Palermo.

The cause of the poverty was simple. The big landowners of Corleone, and towns like it, typically spent their time in Palermo, and leased out their estates on short term contracts to middlemen called gabelloti.

The short leases meant that the gabelloti had to wring money out of the peasants quickly.

Gabelloto / Gabelloti were:

- Ruthless self-made men who readily made enemies.
- Men who had to protect themselves and their assets from bandits and rustlers.

- Frequently in league with, or controlled the bandits.
- Pivotal figures in Sicily's violent economy who were often but not always Mafiosi, in order to get their leases.

In 1893, the oppressed peasants started to combine together in new organisations called Fasci.

The fasci had nothing to do with the anti-democratic movement founded by Benito Mussolini a generation later.

They were very much like a union, to unite the peasants against the landowners and the gabelloti.

The Fasci in Corleone was founded and led by Bernadino Verro. It was one of the first and best organised on the island.

Verro was a bear of a man (aged about 28) who was energetic and absolutely devoted to the cause.

He was an inspiration to other fasci, who copied his socialist demands as their template.

At the heart of the requirement was an even split of the produce, between the proprietor and the peasants who rented small plots of land

Other objectives were to improve the social conditions of the peasant class.

Around this time, Verro had been initiated into the Corleone cosca of the Mafia, without having a full knowledge of the implications.

This was far from typical for the fasci leaders, who were at the vanguard of Italian peasant socialism.

Verro wrote down how he became a Mafioso.

The Mafia had decided to try to harness the fasci, rather than confront it.

As things developed, Verro realised that it had been a mistake to join the Mafia.

In 1894, martial law was declared in Sicily, and this included the dissolution of the fasci.

Violence broke out, and included the troops firing into the crowds.

The Mafia had decided to back the landowners and the state, rather than the fasci.

Verro tried to escape to Tunis, but was arrested in 1894, and tried by a military tribunal. He had been charged with inciting civil war, and for provoking a revolt.

He was found guilty, and given 12 years in prison.

He only served 2 years, and was released in 1896 as part of an amnesty.

In 1907, he was released from a second prison term of 18 months, for the slander of a senior police officer. His key witness had retracted at the last moment.

He was released to a hero's welcome.

Now, 13 years after the repression of the fasci, morale in the peasant movement had never been higher.

A new law made it possible for collectives to borrow money from the Banco di Sicilia, with the sole purpose of renting land directly from the owners.

This process automatically made enemies with the gabelotti who were being cut out of the rural economy.

Verro played a lead role in the Corleone collective, which he knew would put his life in danger.

The Mafia initially tried to bribe Verro into stopping the co-operative from taking the leases.

He resisted, and by 1910, his co-operative had taken charge of 9 estates, freeing hundreds of labourers from near-serfdom in the process.

Verro also faced competition from the Catholic Church, which had a natural antagonism to the new creed of socialism.

It could now be seen that the church and the Mafia had a common ideological ground in their hatred of socialism.

This new alliance posed a new and huge struggle for Verro.

After he made a speech denouncing the "Mafia affiliated with the Catholics", a failed attempt was made on his life.

He claimed that the bullets fired at him stank of "Mafia and incense".

Because the Mafia in Corleone had links with the local MP, the magistrature, and the clergy, Verro was forced to leave Corleone.

However, because of mass peasant support, he returned, to stand as mayor.

Universal male suffrage had been introduced in 1912.

In 1914, he was elected mayor of Corleone.

In May 1914, Italy joined World War 1.

In November 1915, Verro left the town hall, and was gunned down as he entered Via Tribuna.

After he was downed, he was shot a further 4 times in the base of the skull.

He was finally shot in the temple. The state of the corpse was to serve as a warning to others.

Because of the war, the savage murder received very little publicity.

No-one was convicted of the crime.

Over the previous years, the Mafia had tried without success to co-opt Verro, to corrupt him, defeat him politically, smear him, and intimidate him.

Apparently, by 1915, only one instrument remained – murder.

There were many other examples of the Mafia using this final solution to its opposition.

This opposition included 5 good socially committed Catholic priests.

Cesare Mori was a man who became a central player in the history of the Mafia. He had been born near Milan, and had made his career in the police.

He had a driving ambition, which eventually led him to be posted to Sicily in 1903.

From this point onwards, his life was entwined with the history of the Mafia.

By 1915, Mori was deputy of police in the city of Trapani on the western tip of the island.

During the war years, life was chaotic in Sicily, and close to anarchy.

- Over 400,000 Sicilians were drafted.
- Many draft dodgers became bandits in the hills.
- Because of labour shortages, the great estates converted to pasture for rearing animals.
- The war demand on horses, mules and meat, meant that prices increased.

Mori was relentless in his war against crime.

In 1917, he was promoted to chief of the police in the northern city of Turin. Here, he cracked down ruthlessly on the militant socialist workers, and then the right wing student demonstrations.

In both cases, death and injuries resulted.

In Italy, after 1918, there were conflicting pressures between the Socialist, the Catholics and the Nationalists.

The country was in the grip of a desperate economic crisis, and some people were excited by the results of the Russian Revolution of 1917.

Revolution or civil war seemed imminent.

Sicily was similarly placed with its social problems.

Soldiers returning from the war were disgruntled, and wanted reforms, including land reform.

There were also numerous Mafia wars.

These were caused by returning Mafiosi war veterans who had missed out on the profiteering, and who wanted this position to be redressed. They intended to make their presence felt.

The Fascist movement was founded in Milan in March 1919 by journalist and combat veteran, Benito Mussolini.

His aim was to bring the patriotic discipline and aggression of the front to bear on Italy's stunted democracy.

This manifested itself by the dishing out of ferocious beatings to strikers and socialists, across northern and central Italy.

This was approved of by the landowners and industrialists, who were keen to check the progress of the labour movement.

Interestingly, Cesare Mori was made prefect of Bologna in 1921, and confronted black shirted gangs of fascists, much as he would do any other subversives.

This confrontation increased to breaking point, but the impasse evaporated when the government backed down, and Mori was transferred.

This episode left a legacy of bitterness between Mori and the leaders of the Fascist squads.

Mussolini's Fascist Party did not have great numbers in parliament, but it was well organised and had a clear agenda, which appealed in the face of the dithering alternatives.

In October 1922, Mussolini marched on Rome, and challenged the state to either give him power, or put down his movement by force.

In response, he was invited to form a coalition government, and would remain the country's leader for the next 20 years.

After Fascism took power in 1922, the Fascists took revenge by dismissing Mori altogether.

Mori's career was in crisis because he had backed the wrong horse.

He proceeded to make amends, by coming to terms with Fascism, and by demonstrating his admiration for Mussolini.

Once Mussolini (the Duce) had taken power, Sicily suddenly developed a fondness for black shirts and mock Roman salutes, despite not have a strong base of support on the island.

In a short time, Fascism realised that the Mafia in the south would be a useful enemy, as socialism had been in the north.

There could be no better way to accentuate fascism's no nonsense image.

In May 1924, Mussolini visited Sicily with a theatrical display of power.

On the visit, he was persuaded that the Mafia was obstructing the progress of the Fascist Party.

Mussolini was furious when a Mafioso mayor Don Francesco Cuccia, unctuously told him that his bodyguards were totally unnecessary, because he was under Cuccia's protection.

Mussolini returned to Rome and appointed the lobbying Mori, with instructions to return to Trapani.

Cesare Mori was the man that Mussolini had chosen to lead his war on organised crime.

He was expected to cauterize the sore of crime in Sicily – with red hot iron if need be.

Mussolini then almost lost his foothold on power, when some of his thugs kidnapped and murdered a Socialist Party leader.

Opposition inertia allowed the Duce to stabilise the situation, and then to move openly towards putting an end to democracy in Italy.

The Duce was convinced that in Sicily, the dedication and loyalty of so many politicians to the Mafia was preventing the island's loyalty to Fascism.

In January 1925, Prime Minister Benito Mussolini stood up in the Italian parliament, assumed personal responsibility for the violence of his Fascist gangs, and launched a process of suppressing all political opposition.

Mussolini's fascist party was no longer a government, it was a totalitarian regime.

It was in 1926 that Mori became the prefect of Palermo, with full powers to attack the Mafia, and with it, the regime's political enemies.

He immediately began preparations for the campaign's curtain raiser: the siege of Gangi, which was recognised as a bandit headquarters.

The objective was for the Fascist state to out-mafia the Mafia.

Heavy snow was falling on the mountain town. There was a large number of police and carabinieri, as they tightened the cordon and started arresting suspects.

The cordon and the cold weather forced the bandits to back up into Gangi.

Telephone and telegraph wires were cut.

All access roads were blocked.

Gangi, with its poorly lit streets, had previously seemed impregnable, in its lofty isolation.

Now, the streets were brightly lit and teemed with uniformed men who were searching and occupying houses, and making dozens of arrests.

Many of the wanted men had retreated into secret rooms within their houses.

No-one was allowed in or out of Gangi, as the police mounted a series of stunts designed to humiliate the concealed bandits.

Their cattle were confiscated, the best beasts were slaughtered in the town's square, and offered at token prices.

Hostages were taken, including women and children.

Policemen slept in bandit's beds, and rumour suggested that they abused the women.

Then the town crier was put to work:

"Citizens of Gangi! His Excellency Cesare Mori, Prefect of Palermo, has sent the following telegram to the Mayor of Gangi, with the order to make his proclamation public.

"I command all fugitives from justice in this territory, to give themselves up to the authorities within 12 hours of the moment when this ultimatum is read out. Once the deadline has passed, the severest measures will be taken against their families, their possessions, and anyone who has helped them in any way"

Mori had enjoyed the nicknames he had earned in his fight against crime – "the iron prefect" and "the man with hair on his heart".

He was 54 years old, with an imposing build and a deep voice.

He was happy to be a personal enemy of the criminals.

The siege of Gangi was wound up after a few days.

130 fugitives from justice, and some 300 accomplices had been arrested.

The Mafia were on the back foot.

Many Mafiosi were given the maximum 5 years prison sentence, without trial.

When the 5 years were completed, the state issued a decree that gave them 5 more years.

The Sicilian Families were broken up and suffered badly.

In effect, they started to go into hibernation.

Four months after the siege of Gangi, Mori repeated his tactics in the Corleone region.

Over 150 suspects were arrested and dealt with.

The masters of some great estates were appreciative of the effort by the fascists to reduce the power of the Mafia.

Mori often put pressure on the landowners to betray the criminals they had been sheltering for self-survival reasons.

His goal was to impress the population by strength rather than by justice.

Within 3 years of the start of Mori's campaign, some 11,000 people were arrested, 5,000 of them in the province of Palermo alone.

The most prominent trials were carried out in an intimidating atmosphere.

Mori censored the press and endeavoured to create a sense that defending a Mafioso was tantamount to being a Mafioso.

The convictions that fascism needed often followed.

There were also many suicides and murders at this time, which were designed to prevent the spread of damaging information.

An estimated 500 Mafiosi escaped to the USA and to the opportunities presented by Prohibition America. Among these were Carlo Gambino and Joseph

Bonanno, who would go on to become powerful bosses of their own Families in New York City.

During the fascist decades of the 1920's and 1930's, some leading Mafiosi in Sicily still managed to avoid Mori's purges, by being even more efficient with their methods of bribery and corruption.

Giuseppe Genco Russo was one such person, who was left almost unscathed.

As a result of fascism, the Mafia hibernated. It was never eradicated.

In June 1929, after more than 3 years as prefect of Palermo, Cesare Mori received a brief telegram from the Duce, to tell him that his job was finished.

Changes in the political balance of power within the party and the regime had undermined his backing.

He returned to Rome a bitter man.

During the 1930's, the official line was that Mori's task had been completed, and that fascism had beaten the Mafia.

In truth, Sicily sank back into a sump of corruption and factionalism.

Mori's death in 1942 went virtually unreported.

The following year the fascist regime collapsed.

The Mafia's salvation came from the USA. During the same decades in which it had struggled against socialism, fascism, and war in Sicily, the Mafia had become part of the American way of life.

The Sicilian Mafia had given birth to an American version of Cosa Nostra.

1943 – 1950

The Allied invasion
The Separatist movement
The rise of the left wing
The Christian Democrats (DC)
Salvatore Giuliano

In July 1943, the Allies invaded Sicily in the south east. This was known as "Operation Husky".

The British headed towards the mainland, and the Americans advanced north and west.

Villalba was in the very centre of Sicily, and was the town where Don Calogero Vizzini (Don Calo) was the Mafia boss.

Story had it that Lucky Luciano had been released early from prison in the USA in return for arranging the Mafia's help with the invasion.

The story also had it that Luciano was in Sicily to meet Don Calo, who he had chosen to lead the American advance.

Most historians now dismiss this version as fable and folklore.

Luciano was not released from prison until 1946, so there was no American plot to enlist the Mafia as an ally.

A more likely explanation is that the Americans replaced fascist mayors across Sicily by more suitable alternatives, often after consultation with the Catholic Church. Two of Don Calo's brothers were priests, one of his uncles an archpriest, and another was Bishop of Muro Lucano.

Force of personality and local knowledge would help the selection of many Mafiosi mayors.

Having become mayor, Don Calo's first job, like many other mayors, was to expunge all official records of his criminal past.

38 days after the invasion, Sicily was entirely in Allied hands.

At this time, Sicily:

- Was in a dreadful state.
- Had poor food supplies.
- Had a damaged infrastructure.
- Had a soaring crime rate.
- Had many escaped prisoners at large.
- Had a dynamic black market.
- Saw a return to banditry.

These were perfect conditions for the Mafia to operate in, and to control.

The Allies were aware of the existence of the Mafia, but unsurprisingly underestimated their power base.

The Allied view was that left-wing influence had to be avoided at all cost. This policy played into the hands of the Mafia who were happy to exploit this attitude.

The British naively thought their formula used in the Empire would work in these circumstances.

If they secured the landowners and aristocracy, these people would exercise authority on behalf of London.

This policy was plainly not going to work in Mafia dominated Sicily.

It was at this time that the separatist movement started to present itself.

It was supported by the old elite landowners and the Mafia, who both wanted to see leftist policies kept at bay.

This separatist movement picked up considerable momentum.

The new Communist Minister of Agriculture in the new Italian coalition government started to pilot radical land reforms.

These reforms threatened the landowners, the Mafia's protection rackets and the gabelloti.

The battle lines against the Left were being drawn up.

Don Calo was at the forefront of this attack on left-wing politicians and trade unions.

He sparked an incident in Villalba which was given national news coverage.

Mafia methods of conducting business were again seen to triumph, and Don Calo was seen to be very influential, even as a portly 66 year old who appeared to live very simply.

The separatist movement began to fade, as it lost ground to the competing national Christian Democrats (DC) which proposed a regional assembly for Sicily.

Don Calo felt that the DC was the better vehicle for his interests.

The Mafia gradually moved its support to the DC, as did the Vatican.

This was followed by the Americans who saw it as an antidote to the Italian Communist Party, which was the most powerful communist party in Europe by 1947.

In 1948, Italy held its first parliamentary elections since Mussolini established his dictatorial regime. The result was a victory for the DC, who would hold power in Italy for the next 45 years without interruption.

This form of favour based politics, based on patronage and cronyism, was at the heart of its appeal to the Mafia.

The exchanges between politicians and criminals that had been so difficult under fascism, could at last be restored.

"One hand washes the other", as the Sicilian saying goes.

The liaisons between the informal power of the Mafia and the official power of the DC were not shamefaced and in secret. In fact they were intended to be seen as a sign of solidarity.

In 1950, a form of land reform was carried out, but it was very much to the advantage of corrupt DC politicians and the Mafia, all of whom profited.

As the landed gentry disappeared, so the Mafia focussed on the newly available government money and the corrupt politicians who would link them to it.

Although not conclusive, it was believed that Don Calo was the Boss of Bosses in Sicily after the liberation, and that he was succeeded by Giuseppe Genco Russo.

Don Calo died peacefully in Villalba in 1954.

He was reputed to have left a fortune of 1 billion lire, but this cannot be confirmed.

His funeral was attended by huge numbers of both criminals and political dignitaries.

From the 1860's, the Mafia had always had a relationship with bandits.

The most famous and murderous bandit of them all was Salvatore Giuliano.

At the peak of his notoriety he made himself as available to photojournalists as he was elusive to the authorities.

His features were well known, and his life and death both enigmatic.

Up to date, over 40 biographies have been written of him since his death.

There was also Francesco Rosi's 1961 film masterpiece – "Salvatore Giuliano".

It was shot in the mountains around Montelepre, 10 years after his death. This was his stronghold, and local peasants were used as extras.

His life was a tangle between bandits, peasants, the police, the army, politicians, and the media. At the centre of the tangle was the Mafia.

He was born in Montelepre in the mountains, which is some 15 kilometres from Palermo.

At the age of 21, just after the Allied invasion, he became a bandit, after killing a carabinieri.

A dozen of his family were arrested on suspicion of sheltering him.

Early in 1944, he helped them to stage a break out from Monreale Jail. This boosted his reputation, and provided the nucleus of his gang.

He created a Robin Hood myth around himself.

Despite this, his pitiless execution of anyone suspected of betrayal, was also legendary.

The number of his victims has been estimated at a staggering 430.

When kidnapping people for ransom rewards, it was the Mafia who would act as mediators.

Tommaso Buscetta later stated that Giuliano had been initiated.

Unusually for a bandit, he became involved in political ideology.

He joined the separatist movement until it was crushed.

He then joined the struggle against communism. He had been shocked by their 1947 election success for the regional assembly.

The leftist parties had united in a People's Bloc, which gave them 30% of the vote, and made them the biggest single group.

This was the cue for Giuliano to commit his most infamous crime.

The peasants had come together to celebrate on May Day in 1947 in a place called Portella della Ginestra.

The celebration was organised by the Left, and was to mark the return of freedoms that had returned after the fall of Fascism.

Without warning, Giuliano's men opened fire on them. Some were killed, others were injured, and everyone was shocked and traumatised.

The fading of the Communists, and the rise of the DC, turned Giuliano into an anachronism.

He carried on with his activities as a bandit, but his days started to look numbered.

The reasons for the Porta Della Ginestra massacre still remain a mystery. One school of thought was that he was asked to do this by a government minister, who welcomed his war against the Left.

In 1950, Giuliano's body was found in the courtyard of a house in Castelvetrano, which is located outside his mountain realm.

His death remains a total mystery. The carabinieri claimed to have killed him in a furious gun fight.

An investigative reporter proved this to be fiction.

It is more commonly thought that he was shot in bed by his cousin and lieutenant Gaspare Pisciotta. The reason remains a mystery, but may have been based on jealousy.

Pisciotta was given a life sentence for his role in the massacre.

Whilst in prison, he started his autobiography, and his call for a new trial, to face charges for Giuliano's murder, was accepted.

In 1954, and without warning, he died of poisoning in the infamous Ucciardone prison in Palermo.

It was thought that he had put strychnine into his own coffee, believing it to be his TB medicine.

His autobiography vanished.

The mystery surrounding Giuliano was complete.

1950 – 1963

Joe Bannanas
Introduction to the heroin trade
The Sicilian Commission
The Kefauver hearings

During these dates, a new governing body, "The Commission" was established within the Sicilian Mafia, which also began to call itself Cosa Nostra.

It was also during this period that the Sicilian Mafia became involved in the heroin trade, and strengthened its ties with the American version.

Another important area of involvement for the Mafia was the redevelopment of Palermo after the war.

War damage combined with the economic miracle of the late 50's and 60's meant that there were huge opportunities in the construction industry and in redevelopment.

The inevitable massive corruption between the Mafia and the DC politicians, resulted in Palermo being covered in concrete and ugliness.

Many beautiful buildings were lost to this ferocious and unprincipled development, which became known as the sack of Palermo.

Giuseppe "Joe Bannanas" Bonanno had the longest reign of any of the bosses of the five New York Mafia Families.

He was born in 1905 in Castellammare del Golfo, and as a 19 year old, fled Mussolini's Italy in the 1920's.

He fought alongside Salvatore Maranzano (also from his birth town), against Joe "the Boss" Masseria, and was made the boss of his own Family following the Lucky Luciano pacification of the New York Families in 1931.

For over 3 decades he led the Brooklyn based Bonanno Family.

Whilst he was boss, it remained the most Sicilian of the New York Families, and Sicilian remained their first language.

Along with Magaddinos in Buffalo, to whom Joe was related by blood, the Bonanno Family maintained close links with the Mafia back in his birth town.

In 1957, Joe Bonanno returned to Sicily. This visit marked a turning point for Cosa Nostra in both countries.

Two significant things happened.

- The US Mafiosi franchised out heroin trafficking to their Sicilian cousins.
- The Sicilian Mafia created a commission based on the US version.

These two events set the stage for all the drama of Mafia history over the next 4 decades.

These actions were both business and political.

In America, the drug trade had opened up, but drugs were perceived to be a dirty business, even by those politicians and judiciary who protected the Mafia.

In 1951, Democrat Senator Estes Kefauver, conducted televised hearings in which he questioned the heads of the Mafia.

The Kefauver Hearings aroused a drugs scare and condemnation, despite the fact that J. Edgar Hoover, director of the FBI, refused to accept the existence of the Mafia!

"Kefauver" led to the introduction of the Narcotics Central Act of 1956, which stipulated a 40 year maximum prison term for drug related offences.

This pressure on the American Mafia was probably the reason for Bonanno's visit to Sicily. They had been forced to crack down on their American activities, even if this was for cosmetic purposes.

At the same time (1956-57) the American Mafia's most important offshore base (Cuba) for narcotics smuggling, was slipping from their grip.

It had fallen to Castro by 1959.

It is not therefore "rocket science" to deduce that Bonanno's 1957 trip to Sicily was designed to find the following for its narcotics interests.

- A trustworthy source of manpower.
- A partner to which it could franchise out a business that had become too damaging to run "hands on".
- A new transhipment base.

Sicilian politicians were not as sensitive about narcotics, because it hadn't yet become a big social problem in Italy.

It would also be easy for Sicilians to collect refined heroin from the South of France, where it was processed.

Bonanno's meetings were attended by other American Mafiosi as well as high ranking Sicilians.

By 1957, the Sicilian Mafia was already sending morphine to America via fruit crates.

This convention in Sicily however, marked the beginning of a new era of heroin cooperation. This was to be the focus of future business.

Don Calo had been succeeded by Genco Russo who was also present at these meetings.

Genco Russo was known as "boss of bosses" for the whole of Sicily. This was later refuted by Buscetta, who said that such a title could only be held by a Mafioso in Palermo – not a small town in central Sicily.

Bonanno's idea of a Commission was actioned by:

- Tommaso Buscetta.
- Gaetano "Tano" Badalamenti.
- Salvatore "Little Bird" Greco.

They became a 3 man constitutional working party.

All three went on to become major narcotics dealers.

The Commission's crucial function would be to make rulings on the murders of "men of honour".

Its creation had epoch-making political implications. In effect, the power of life and death over other Mafiosi was designed to be taken out of the hands of the Family bosses.

Buscetta incidentally never rose above the rank of soldier because he always had a roving commission regarding Mafia business interests. He was not a territorial operator.

Interestingly Lucky Luciano had been territorial when in America.

On expulsion in 1946, rather than settle in his native Palermo, he settled in Naples and conducted his business from there.

Buscetta was keen to see the Commission reduce the power of the Bosses, and give more commercial autonomy and freedom to individual Mafiosi.

The Commission was supposed to make the Mafia more like an association of autonomous men of honour.

It is difficult to understand exactly why Joe Bonanno, a Family boss, would promote this kind of restructuring of the political machine.

As it happened, in the early 80's, the Commission metamorphosed into exactly the reverse of what Buscetta had hoped for.

It became an instrument of dictatorship for the Corleonesi.

1962 – 1969

The 1ˢᵗ Mafia war
The Ciaculli bomb
Joe Valachi
The Antimafia

In late 1962 and early 1963, there was a spate of killings within the Mafia in Palermo, which had all the signs of a power struggle.

But internal conflict in the Mafia is never predictable, because within Cosa Nostra, deceit and politics are as important as guns and bombs.

This war proved to be a mystery. It was not felt to be a battle between the "old" and the "new" Mafia, despite the leading combatants.

On one side was:

- Salvatore "Little Bird" Greco, who was part of a Mafia dynasty.
- Luciano Leggio, who had become head of the Corleone Family in the 1950's.

On the other side was:

- Angelo La Barbero, who was Boss of Palermo-Centre.
- Salvatore La Barbero, his brother.

- Pietro Torretta, ex Salvatore Giuliano bandit, and then Boss of Uditore.
- Tommaso Buscetta.

The 1st Mafia war was started when someone cheated on a drug deal in 1962.

Both sides were part of a consortium that had financed a consignment of heroin from Egypt that was delivered to southern Sicily.

It was forwarded via Calcedonio Di Pisa to New York, but when it arrived, they found they had been short measured.

The Commission cleared Di Pisa of theft, but he was still shot dead in Palermo.

Other members of his Family were soon attacked.

Then in January 1963, the retaliation started when Salvatore La Barbero became the victim of a "white shotgun" killing (i.e. he was killed, but the body disappeared). Only his car was found, burned out.

Brother Angelo was determined to continue the war after his brother's death.

He made a failed attempt on "Little Bird" Greco, when he bombed his house.

Then Greco's ally, the Cinisi boss was killed.

Then La Barbero was badly shot whilst in a residential street in Milan. He miraculously survived.

When the Mafia spread beyond Sicily, the issue moved up the whole nation's political agenda.

It is thought that Buscetta and Torretta both started on La Barbero's side, but changed when they thought Greco was going to win.

Nevertheless, with La Barbero shot so badly, and arrested, Buscetta and Torretta considered themselves to be the natural successors of Palermo-Centre.

Torretta proposed himself as capo with Buscetta as underboss.

The Greco's were opposed to this as they distrusted Buscetta.

This protracted dispute reignited hostilities between Torretta and Buscetta on one side, against the Grecos on the other.

This started to gain momentum.

The Ciaculli bomb in June 1963 was intended to destroy the Grecos, but was thwarted by a puncture in the car that became the bomb.

It occurred in Greco dynasty territory and was close to Villabate.

It marked a turning point in Mafia history.

An Alpha Romeo Giulietta was reported as abandoned. It was suspected of being a car bomb since another Giulietta had exploded earlier in Villabate, killing 2 people.

After two hours, the police and bomb disposal experts had diffused a large bomb. Then, on opening the boot of the car, it exploded and killed 7 officials.

Previously, the Mafia had only killed each other. This was the first serious mass killing of officials, and could no longer be ignored.

The police made more than 40 arrests in Ciaculli and Villabate, and confiscated a large number of weapons.

This was the beginning of the biggest round up of Mafiosi since Cesare Mori.

Over 100,000 people attended the funeral of the victims, in Palermo Cathedral.

The political pressure to take the Mafia problem seriously became huge.

This outrage had marked a historic point of no return.

The nation could no longer be in denial about the size of the Mafia problem, and its challenge to the state.

The Ciaculli bomb also brought to an end what became known as the "1st Mafia war".

The crackdown that followed scattered Mafiosi across both Italy and the world.

Yet to this day, nobody really knows for certain who planted the bomb. It follows that no-one was ever charged for the offence, although Buscetta was suspected.

Buscetta suggested that a third party, Michele Cavataio, had killed Di Pisa, in the knowledge that it would cause a war between the two factions.

At this time, there was also developing a conflict between the Mafia's role as a shadow government, and the business interests of its members – between the territorial structure of the cosche, and the highly profitable smuggling networks.

At about this time, Robert Kennedy was putting huge pressure on Cosa Nostra in America.

As attorney general, he was working on the Senate Labour Rackets Committee. He was tackling the mob head on and was using tax law as his main weapon.

Under Kennedy, convictions trebled between 1961 and 1963, and then nearly doubled again in 1964.

It was these laws that had earlier trapped Capone.

In 1962, faced with the electric chair, Gambino soldier Joe Valachi turned pentito.

As a result J. Edgar Hoover's FBI started to take the Mafia seriously for the first time.

In 1959 in the New York office of the FBI, there were 400 agents investigating American Communism, and only 4 working on organized crime!

In 1963, the number was increased to 140.

In 1964, the FBI obtained recordings of the Teamster union boss Jimmy Hoffa having discussions with the Detroit Mafia.

This pressure on the American Mafia reduced its influence in Sicily.

Angelo La Barbero had become a little isolated when his ally Lucky Luciano died of a heart attack in Naples airport. Both had an interest in narcotics.

In the summer of 1963, after close to 2,000 arrests, the Sicilian Mafia went into hiding and the Commission dissolved itself.

The Families disbanded.

Protection money was not collected.

Mafia crimes dropped to almost zero.

A number of bosses fled abroad.

"Little Bird" Greco went to Switzerland and then to Venezuela.

Buscetta went to Switzerland, Mexico, Canada, and then to the US.

As Luciano had done when he was expelled from America in 1946, many Sicilian Mafiosi simply changed the direction of their careers within the organization.

From becoming power syndicate criminals – statesmen of the Mafia shadow government, they became enterprise syndicate leaders – international paramilitary business men.

As they did so, the Italian political system once again became the chief player in the Mafia's history.

Up until the Ciaculli bomb (1963), there were very few voices raised against the Mafia.

Both the Catholic Church and the DC denied its very existence.

Any opposition had come from the left wing newspaper L'Ora, which was hounded by the Mafia for its investigative reporting.

Its offices were bombed and some of its reporters were murdered.

Only the left wing and the communists seemed to be concerned, and therefore became the Mafia's historic enemies.

Immediately after the Ciaculli bomb incident, a parliamentary enquiry called "The Antimafia" began at a brisk pace.

It slowed to a gentle amble, and lasted 13 years.

Changes of personnel and factional tussles reduced the effectiveness and achievements of The Antimafia until it finally ran aground with nearly 40 fat volumes.

It revealed a great deal about the workings of the Mafia, but didn't lead to a concerted action plan.

In 1968, 117 of the combatants of the 1st Mafia war were put on trial in Cantanzaro in Calabria. The verdicts were produced in the December and La Barbero was sentenced to 22 years in jail for his role.

In 1975, he was stabbed to death in the prison yard.

If The Antimafia was seen as a political anticlimax, Cantanzaro was seen as a judicial anticlimax – not because the jury had been corrupted, but because the Mafia had been its usual slippery intimidating self.

A few of the lead players however received long sentences.

- Torretta got 27 years.
- La Barbera got 22 years.
- Greco (in absentia) got 10 years.
- Buscetta (in absentia) got 14 years.

Most of the rest were acquitted or received short sentences.

In 1969, Mafiosi dressed as policemen, gunned down and killed Michele Cavataio, the Mafioso blamed by Buscetta for starting the 1st Mafia war.

This killing marked the end of the 1st Mafia war, and added credibility to the Buscetta version of events.

Pentiti later confirmed that "Little Bird" Greco had instigated the execution after he had accepted Buscetta's theory.

1970 – 1982

Michele Navarra
Luciano Leggio
Heroin becomes big business
The arrival of Falcone
Michele Sindona
Roberto Calvi
P2
The 2nd Mafia war
Salvatore Toto Riina

Luciano Leggio was both volatile and malevolent, and had a look that struck fear even into the hearts of the Mafiosi.

He reinvented Mafia tactics that were a new combination of old methods.

As boss of the Corleonesi, he developed a system for dominating the Sicilian Mafia during the new climate of The Antimafia years.

Luciano Leggio was born into poverty on a farm just outside Corleone in 1925. He was one of 10 children.

After the Allied invasion, Leggio the petty thief was drafted into the Mafia by Michele Navarra who was boss of the Corleonesi, and also a physician in Corleone.

Leggio's first job was to guard a Corleone estate. As a 23 year old he brutally murdered the local trade unionist Placido Rizzotto.

Although there were witnesses, he was never convicted.

He absconded after the murder and was a fugitive from justice for over 25 years.

Leggio's life of almost permanent concealment was to set a pattern for other Corleonesi bosses.

He was not only concealed from the forces of law and order, but also from rival Mafiosi.

The invisibility was to become part of the new model of Mafia power.

Whilst on the run, Leggio made a challenge, and then killed Michele Navarra.

This move was very daring because the evil Navarra:

- Represented a kind of Mafia stability.
- Was president of the Corleone peasants association.
- Was a trustee of the farmer's union.
- Was an inspector for the region's health insurance scheme.
- Placed his friends on a host of influential quangos.
- Controlled a significant package of votes for the DC.
- Had support from other bosses in the region.
- Had contacts in the U.S.
- Was known locally as "Our Father" and had considerable prestige.

Leggio proceeded to press his advantage with some very high profile killings.

His coup was violent, but successful.

It showed that the Mafia's military wing was always more powerful than its political wing.

This became a characteristic tactic adopted by the Corleonesi thereafter.

Leggio's 5 year pursuit of domination in Corleone was interrupted by the Ciaculli bomb and by The Antimafia.

In 1969, 64 of the combatants in the war between the Leggiani and the Navarriani came to trial.

All were acquitted for the traditional reasons of intimidation.

Mafia business then resumed in earnest.

Two of Leggio's men were involved in the killing of Michele Cavataio, also known as "the Cobra".

One of them was Bernardo (the tractor) Provenzano, who later became boss of bosses.

Leggio's status was confirmed when the Commission was reconstituted.

Its new provisional composition included:

- Gaetano "Tano" Badalamenti, a major drug dealer with good USA contacts.
- Stefano Bontate, capo of the largest Family in Palermo.
- Luciano Leggio, who was usually represented by his under boss, Toto "Shorty" Riina.

This commission was different because all 3 were capos – the previous one excluded capos.

Their new positions made them the top 3 in the Sicilian Mafia.

In 1974, the commission became fully operative.

Leggio achieved his high position because he was not only the boss in Corleone; he had extended his influence to Palermo where it really counted.

Palermo was where he spent most of his time in hiding.

It was here that he developed close relationships with the combatants of the 1st Mafia war – La Barbera, Buscetta, Greco, Cavataio, and Torretta.

Palermo was the place where the Mafia:

- Had its roots.
- Had its power concentrated.
- Would fight the 2nd Mafia war.

Leggio was eventually arrested in Milan in 1974 as a result of wire-tapping. He was 49 years old and was given a life sentence for the slaying of Michele Navarra.

In March 1973, Leonardo Vitale became a pentito as a result of undergoing a religious crisis.

He was a 32 year old Mafioso whose uncle was his capo.

He himself had become a capodecina (head of 10).

He confessed to a number of crimes including murder.

He also explained how a Mafia family was organised, who was in his own Family, and the existence of the Commission.

It was a total exposure, including how his uncle had groomed him for initiation.

He was psychiatrically examined because he seemed unstable, and the prosecution wanted to know if he would be able to cope with the pressures of a court case.

In 1977 he faced trial. Of the 28 defendants, only Vitale and his uncle were convicted.

He received 25 years, but was released in 1984 after serving only 7 years.

Within a few months he was shot twice in the head whilst returning from church with his mother and sister.

Vitale's profoundly important insight into the nature of the Mafia was subsequently completely ignored by the authorities.

Also in the 1970's, Italian democracy faced its darkest days since the fall of Fascism.

Battle lines were being draw up between neo-Fascist groups– including those who were in the Italian secret service – on one side, and militant left-wing groups that included the Communists, on the other.

It was thought that a series of terrorist outrages would prepare the ground for a right-wing coup d'etat.

The right-wing itself was a reaction to the threat from the left-wing which included the workers movements, the Communists, and the militant Red Brigades.

The extreme Red Brigade murdered policemen, magistrates, entrepreneurs, journalists, and even Communists who they thought had "sold out".

The Mafia was recruited to the right-wing cause. Having said that, the Mafia could be counted on to support the victor of any such political dispute or conflict. As stated before, the Mafia will always follow the money, and not be handicapped by a moral argument.

It was at this time in the early 70's that a generation of younger magistrates spearheaded a drive to reform the sclerotic legal system.

There was a slow transformation in Italy's legal system that would later help in the struggle against Cosa Nostra.

In 1978, the Red Brigades kidnapped the most prominent member of the DC, former Prime Minister Aldo Moro. His entire escort and his driver were murdered in the assault.

55 days later he was killed and his body put in the boot of a car.

These national events had relegated any Mafia news onto the back pages of the newspapers.

On the same day that Aldo Moro was murdered in Rome, Peppino Impastato was murdered in Cinisi near Palermo.

His father was a Mafioso, whereas Peppino was a left-wing activist who despised Cosa Nostra.

The local boss was Don Tano Badalamenti who was on the provisional Commission in 1970.

Peppino's mother warned him of the danger he was creating for himself.

In May 1978 Peppino was kidnapped.

He was beaten and tortured before being dumped on a rail track, with dynamite strapped to his torso.

His body was scattered over a 300 meter radius by the explosion.

Over 20 years later, a parliamentary commission criticised the slipshod investigation into his murder.

As a result of later pentiti, Tano Badalamenti was eventually committed for trial in 1999.

In 2002, he was given a life sentence for ordering Impastato's murder.

Peppino's mother, Felicia Bartolotta Impastato, gave a great insight into the role of women in the Mafia Family, and after the 2002 trial, she still bravely took an anti-Mafia stance. She must have been a woman of great courage, considering that she knew the price to be paid by people who offended the Mafia.

In 1970, because of their recent trials, many of the bosses had lost a great deal of money. Their coffers were empty.

Then suddenly within a couple of years, they were millionaires.

The history of Cosa Nostra in the 70's rides on a flood tide of heroin profits.

And it was that flood tide that ultimately led to the bloodiest war in the Mafia's history.

In 1970, the Grecos and Tano Badalamenti were still comfortable, but the rest needed money quickly, none more than the Corleonesi.

They initially turned to child kidnapping as a way of meeting their basic needs and accumulating capital.

There was also a boom in tobacco smuggling, centred on Naples.

This was followed by the Mafia's dedication to heroin.

President Nixon had declared war on drugs in the U.S.

By causing the closure of the Corsican-run refineries in Marsailles, the Nixon administration created the opportunity for Sicily to become the new base for the crucial phase in heroin's long journey from the poppy fields of Afghanistan, to the streets of America.

In 1975, a Turkish drugs and arms dealer, who had been a main supplier to the Marseilles refineries, approached Cosa Nostra directly.

Soon afterwards, heroin laboratories sprang up across western Sicily, staffed initially by refugees from Marseilles.

In 1977 heroin addiction in America and Europe saw a huge leap as the Sicilian refineries came on stream and dominated the market.

Not content with this, the Sicilians also wanted to control the distribution network.

They collaborated with the American Cosa Nostra in the importation of heroin via the importation of foodstuffs.

The Pizza Connection case in the USA in 1986 would prove that pizza parlours were the Mafia's transnational heroin distribution network.

By 1982, the Mafia were controlling about 80% of the refining, shipping, and distribution of heroin used in the north eastern US.

By this time, Cosa Nostra in Sicily had become wealthier and more powerful than ever before.

The power balance between the two arms of Cosa Nostra had changed, and the Sicilians could no longer be patronised.

The Bonanno Family in Brooklyn became a Sicilian colony and heroin terminal.

The Sicilians were getting more involved not only with the enterprise syndicate, but also with the American power syndicate.

In 1979, a Sicilian actually took over as boss of the Bonanno Family for 2 years. He is said to have stepped down only because he found it difficult doing business in English.

The kinship between the 2 countries continued during the 70's as cousins across the Atlantic continued to marry.

Drug trafficking requires a huge network of different skills. Not everyone will be a Mafiosi.

Many tasks are outsourced to others in order to confuse the picture and to keep the Mafia more remote from prosecution.

Dealers are not usually Mafiosi, but have their protection.

In 1978 Giovanni Falcone arrived at the Palace of Justice in Palermo. His early career was in the bankruptcy court where he developed his skills of hunting down obscure financial records.

Within 2 years the "Falcone method" produced a breakthrough in a case that went to the heart of Cosa Nostra's transatlantic drug business.

It was 1st applied to a big heroin smuggling case in 1980, after Falcone was transferred to the criminal investigative office of Palermo.

In 1982, he secured 74 convictions in the heroin case: a prodigious success on an island where the terrorising of witnesses, judges, and juries had caused the failure of innumerable previous cases.

He was also working on a fraud and murder case in Milan that threatened to expose the very worst of Italian society, in the form of corruption, Mafia influence, and anti-democratic conspiracy at the highest levels of the political and financial institutions. The case centred on Michele Sindona who was:

- The most influential financial figure in Italy.
- In charge of one of the biggest banks in the US.
- In charge of the Vatican's foreign investments.
- A major funder of DC politicians.
- Strongly suspected of laundering money for Cosa Nostra.

In 1974, his empire collapsed amid fraud charges. Then he:

- Fled to the USA.
- In 1979, commissioned a Mafioso to kill the lawyer in charge of liquidating his Italian affairs.
- Staged his own hoax kidnapping.
- Arranged for himself to be anaesthetised and shot in the left thigh, to add credibility to his abduction.
- Eventually gave himself up to the FBI.
- Died in prison in 1986 after drinking coffee that had been laced with cyanide.

In 1982 another disgraced banker, Roberto Calvi, was found dead, hanging under Blackfriars Bridge in London.

Calvi had:

- Risen rapidly, and was head of Banco Ambrosiano which he built into Italy's largest private bank.
- Close ties to the Vatican bank via Archbishop Marcinkus.
- Channelled funds to governing political parties.
- Suffered a financial collapse.
- Attempted to save himself by blackmailing politicians.

In 2002, the case was re-examined and it was eventually judged that Calvi had not committed suicide, but had been murdered.

A pentito claimed that he had been laundering money for the Corleonesi, just as Sindona had done for the Inzerillo / Gambino / Spatola / Bontate group.

Both of God's bankers were disposed of because they had proved unreliable.

They were both also members of a Masonic Lodge known as P2 (Propaganda Due)

In 1981, a list of 962 members of P2 were found in the office of Grand Master, Licio Gelli.

Membership included:

- The entire leadership of the secret services.
- 44 members of parliament.
- A slew of senior business men.

- Military figures.
- Policemen.
- Civil servants.
- Journalists.

The parliamentary inquiry into P2 concluded that its aim had been to pollute public life, and to undermine democracy, although not all members would have understood this.

The exact extent of P2's influence is still unclear, but it is thought by some to have extended into the Roman Catholic Church, and had a role in the demise of Pope John Paul 1st. This proposition was fully explored in the fascinating book IN GOD'S NAME by DAVID YALLOP.

When Mafiosi joined Masonic lodges for networking purposes, their loyalty was never in doubt. They had but one loyalty!

It's now known that the 2 richest men in Sicily during the 80's were both members of the Mafia and of the Masons.

They were the Salvo cousins who had a tax collecting scam, and one for diverting EU and Italian government subsidies.

The corrupt short circuit between the Salvos, the Mafia, and sections of the DC, deformed the whole Sicilian political system.

In 1982, Judge Falcone subjected the Salvo empire to an audit.

This marked the beginning of his head-on confrontation with Cosa Nostra.

The Second Mafia War of 1981-83 was a brutal affair, that amounted to a savage cull.

There were two factions:

The Corleone faction was headed by:

- Luciano Leggio(in jail).
- Salvatore Toto "Shorty" Riina.
- Bernardo "The Tractor" Provenzano.
- Michele "The Pope" Greco.
- Nitto "The Hunter" Santapaola.

The Anti-Corleone faction was headed by:

- Don "Tano" Badalamenti.
- Stefano Bontate.
- Salvatore Totuccio Inzerillo (a big heroin dealer).
- Tommaso Buscetta.

The war did not come unannounced.

A full 3 years before the slaughter began, the carabinieri were given an accurate map of the battle lines and a briefing of the tactics of the winners – the Corleonesi.

This was provided in 1978 by Giuseppe Di Cristina, who was boss of a cosca in central-southern Sicily, and who had been part of the 1969 execution squad for "the Cobra"(Michele Cavataio).

He related how Leggio had still run his Family whilst serving the first 4 years of his life sentence in jail.

He estimated that Riina and Provenzano (known as "the beasts") were each guilty of at least 40 murders.

Di Cristina also claimed that Leggio was responsible for the Rome kidnapping of Eugene Paul Getty III, the 17 year old grandson of Paul Getty.

The boy was held for 5 months before a ransom was paid. A lock of his hair and his ear had been sent to a newspaper as proof of the kidnappers' strength of mind.

The Corleonesi were implementing a long term strategy by:

- Encircling the opposing faction by winning over all of the smaller Families.
- Infiltrating the enemy Families.
- Building a secret army by initiating Mafiosi without informing the other bosses. This was outside the general rules of the Mafia.

A few weeks after these revelations in 1978, Di Cristina was shot dead in the outskirts of Palermo, in the territory of Inzerillo.

No-one was prosecuted.

Again it was shown that parallel to the authority of the state, there is a more incisive and efficient power that acts, moves, makes money, kills, and even makes judgements – all behind the back of the authorities.

Subsequent pentiti confirmed that the Corleonesi strategy to dominate both Cosa Nostra and the Commission, started just after the formation of the Bontate / Badalamenti / Leggio triumvirate of 1970.

At that time the Corleonesi were militarily strong but financially weak.

They carried out a lot of kidnappings and distributed the ransom money amongst the neediest Palermo Families, after The Antimafia purge.

They focussed on the Cosa Nostra power structure, rather than on new business ventures.

A number of the kidnappings were designed to humiliate Badalamenti and Bontate.

In 1977, the Corleonesi expelled Badalamenti from Cosa Nostra, on the pretext that he was getting rich behind the backs of the others bosses.

The Corleonesi now controlled the Commision which Badalamenti had presided over since it was re-established in 1974.

They appointed Michelle "the Pope" Greco as the titular head, to replace him.

Around this time, the leadership of the Corleonesi was passed from Luciano Leggio, who was serving a life sentence, to his disciple Toto Riina, who was assisted by Bernardo Provenzano.

As Leggio had been a volatile "hot head", so Riina was a calm, humble, placid, smiling person, who never lost his temper. He was of course, utterly ruthless.

The Anti-Corleone faction were still very wealthy and powerful, but their power was mostly outside Cosa Nostra.

The Corleonesi however had created massive power "within" Cosa Nostra. They had won over both the Families and the Commission.

They had dominated the power syndicate, rather than the short term enterprise syndicate activities.

Buscetta was released from jail in 1980.

He read the game, and in January 1981 took a plane to Brazil, intending never to return.

On April 23rd 1981, whilst many Englishmen were celebrating St George's day, the Corleonesi under Riina's leadership, began their cull.

In less than 2 years, as many as 1,000 people were murdered by shooting or strangulation. Their bodies were dissolved in acid, buried in concrete, dumped at sea, or cut up and fed to the pigs.

This was the bloodiest conflict in Mafia history. It was not so much a war, but more a campaign of extermination.

Bontate was slaughtered in his car at traffic lights.

Just over 2 weeks later, Inzerillo was shot down getting into his car.

With Badalamenti in the USA and Buscetta in Brazil, the Corleonesi had decapitated the opposition.

People waited for a reaction from the Anti-Corleone faction, but what happened instead was a mass execution of their followers by the Corleonesi.

The Corleonesi were pitting overwhelming military force against wealth and political influence.

It was no contest!

In the following weeks and months:

- 200 men from the opposition were killed in the Palermo area.
- There were many "white shotgun" murders (no bodies were found).
- Most of the Corleonesi enemies were killed before they knew they were in danger - often betrayed by men in their own Family, who had defected to the Corleonesi.

- Sometimes Mafiosi were killed by their own Family, and presented as sacrificial offerings to the victor.
- The Families of murdered bosses were handed over to Corleonesi loyalists.
- The American Cosa Nostra was told to find and eliminate Buscetta and all Mafiosi from the losing faction.
- The Corleonesi proceeded to kill all Mafiosi whose loyalty was even remotely in doubt.
- With stunning brutality, any friends or family were cut down if they might plausibly offer shelter to the losers. When Salvatore Contorno escaped execution, an incredible 35 members of his family were then murdered.
- After Riina had disposed of his enemies and fence sitters, he then turned on his own allies who had shown signs of independent thinking. This included the underboss of the Ciaculli Family – Pino "the Shoe" Greco, who had been a leading Corleonesi assassin. He had been part of the squad that killed Bontate and Inzerillo. In 1985 he was shot dead by his own men, on the orders of Riina.
- A dictatorship over Sicily's Cosa Nostra had been achieved.

1983 – 1992

Tommaso Buscetta
The maxi-trial
The Falcone years
The Borsellino years

Up until this point the Mafia had not aggressively targeted notable members of the establishment.

This began to change under the Corleonesi dictatorship of Toto Riina.

General Carlo Alberto Dalla Chiesa was made the new prefect of Palermo, with the role of confronting the Mafia.

Within a few months, Chiesa, his wife and escort were all slaughtered.

The battle against the Mafia was being fought by a heroic minority of magistrates and police, supported by a minority of politicians, administrators, journalists, and members of the public. It was never the "Italian State" as such, that took on Cosa Nostra.

In July 1983, a car bomb in central Palermo killed Falcone's boss, Rocco Chinnici, the chief investigating magistrate.

Killed with him were his 2 bodyguards and the concierge where he lived.

Antonino Caponnetto, who was nearing retirement, volunteered to replace Chinnici. He then proceeded to live for four and a half years in the carabanieri barracks, for his own protection.

Significantly, he decided to create a pool of specialised anti-Mafia magistrates.

This comprised Giovanni Falcone, Paolo Borsellino, Giuseppe Di Lello, and Leonardo Guarnotta.

This team started to have stunning successes.

In 1984, Tommaso Buscetta became a pentito, and 366 arrest warrants were issued as a result.

Buscetta had been born in Palermo and was the youngest of 17 children.

Rather unusually for a Mafioso, he was a womaniser and bigamist. He also had at least 12 children of his own.

Amongst the victims of the Corleonesi slaughter, Buscetta lost 2 sons, a brother, a nephew, a brother-in-law, and a son-in-law. The papers had dubbed him "the boss of two worlds" because of his interests on both sides of the Atlantic. When the Corleonesi mounted their assault, neither of his worlds were safe for him anymore. Buscetta had been arrested in Brazil. When he was extradited to Italy, he tried to commit suicide by swallowing the strychnine that he always carried with him. He survived the attempt – just. On recovering, Buscetta decided to spill the beans about the secret society to which he had been initiated when he was 17. And it was to Giovanni Falcone, and to him alone, that he wanted to speak.

Buscetta provided Falcone, for the 1st time, with access to the Sicilian Mafia from the inside.

After many hours of interviews, Falcone and his team developed their understanding of the organisation, and patiently mapped the connections between faces, names, and crimes.

They assembled a completely new picture of its command structure, methods and mindset.

It is hard to now realise how much was NOT known about the Mafia, before Tommaso Buscetta sat down with Giovanni Falcone.

Falcone then set out to prove that the Mafia was a single unified structure - described as the Buscetta theorem.

The Corleonesi responded by killing pentiti and their relatives.

Some very good police officers were also killed. These officers felt that they were not well enough supported by the state authorities, and that they were isolated.

Falcone and Borsellino were about the same age, and were both brought up in the same small central area of Palermo – la Kasa.

Falcone's father was a chemist.

Borsellino's was a pharmacist.

They were both devoted to duty and had an unshakable faith in justice.

Falcone had left-wing sympathies, whereas Borsellino was right-wing and had a much stronger Catholic faith.

Both men were brought up under a code of duty, church, and patriotism.

Both men also drew strength from Sicily's increasing anti-Mafia movement. This included the voice of the Cardinal Primate, who not only used the word "mafia", but also denounced the state's inaction in the face of slaughter.

In addition, Palermo's DC mayor, elected in 1985, was a vocal opponent of the Mafia.

The famous maxi-trial opened in February 1986 and lasted for almost 2 years.

It took place in a massive floodlit bunker abutting the Ucciardone prison, where a specially built courtroom was housed.

474 men faced charges, but 119 were still on the run.

The most notable of those on the run were Luciano Leggio's "beasts" – "Shorty" Riina and "The Tractor" Provenzano.

Leggio himself was in court where, with others, he was housed in one of the 30 cages that were positioned around the periphery of the court.

Public opinion about the objectives or the outcome of the trial was very mixed.

Doubts were cast over the validity of pentiti evidence.

The verdicts of the maxi-trial were announced in December 1987.

The results were:

- Of the 474 on trial, 114 were acquitted.
- 360 were given 2,665 years jail between them.
- The court upheld the "Buscetta theorem".
- Luciano Leggio was one of the acquitted because it couldn't be proved that he had been giving orders from behind bars whilst in jail. He was of course still serving a life sentence.

There followed 2 more maxi-trials, and then an important pentito, Antonio Calderone, gave evidence that launched the 4th maxi-trial.

In 1988, 160 arrests were made for this trial.

All this time, the Mafia believed that they would still be able to buy successful appeals.

New legislation freed many men judged guilty, until their appeals were heard.

In 1990, the Palermo Court of Appeal reversed some of the maxi-trial convictions, and also failed to uphold the central plank of the "Buscetta theorem".

There was at this time an insidious opposition to Falcone from within the judiciary.

The verdicts were referred to Italy's National Supreme Court of Appeal.

After the maxi-trial verdict, Antonino Caponnetto decided to retire as head of the anti-Mafia pool, and return to Florence.

Falcone was the obvious candidate to succeed him, however due to internal politics the job went to Antonino Meli.

This seemed an odd decision, since Meli had never even investigated any Mafia cases.

Falcone was humiliated, devastated, and very afraid for his life.

He realised that if the state didn't back him, Cosa Nostra could well take advantage of his vulnerability.

Meli's method of operation suggested that he was sabotaging all that the anti-Mafia pool stood for, and all that they had achieved.

In 1989, a sports bag filled with dynamite was placed outside the beach house that Falcone had rented. This threat was successfully dealt with.

His life was not in immediate danger, but internal politics within the judicial system was making life almost impossible for both Falcone and Borsellino.

In 1991, the fate of the anti-Mafia movement dramatically reversed.

Following the fall of the Berlin Wall in 1989, the political dynamics changed, and suddenly reform was in the air.

Falcone was invited to become the Director of Penal Affairs, with the responsibility for coordinating the fight against organised crime at a national level

He proceeded to set up 2 national bodies:

- The DIA to unite the efforts of law enforcement agencies. It became a sort of Italian FBI.
- The DNA – a national anti-Mafia prosecutors office which coordinated the efforts of 26 district anti-Mafia offices around the country. Each office was obliged by law to keep a computer database on organised crime.

In the meantime Riina was murdering members of the judiciary as the results of the maxi-trial appeal were awaited from the Supreme Court of Appeal.

Thankfully in January 1992, Italy's Supreme Court of Appeal confirmed the 3 central contentions of Falcone's and Borsellino's original prosecution case. Notably:

- Cosa Nostra was a single unified organisation.
- The Commission was responsible for the murders carried out by its members.
- Evidence from pentiti was valid for prosecutions.

As a result, the "Buscetta theorem" was proved, and Cosa Nostra bosses faced life sentences.

It was the greatest defeat for the Mafia since it began in 1860.

Falcone was riding high.

In response however, the Corleonesi put their death squads onto the investigating magistrates.

1992 – 2010

The murder of Falcone
The murder of Borsellino
The suicide of Rita Atria
Gian Carlo Caselli
Leoluca Bagarella
Giulio Andreotti
Bernardo Provenzano

It was only a few months after the verdicts were given from the Supreme Court of Appeal.

On May 23rd 1992, on a short stretch of motorway that leads to Palermo from the city's airport, and just before the turn off to the small town of Capaci, leading anti-Mafia investigating magistrate Giovanni Falcone and his wife were murdered by means of an enormous roadside bomb. Some of their escort were also killed.

The device was activated by Giovanni Brusca, a stocky, bearded, young "man of honour".

In murdering Falcone, the Sicilian Mafia had removed its most dangerous enemy.

The Capaci bomb not only brought Italy to a standstill, it also triggered the demise of any romantic myths associated with the Mafia.

It's worth noting that the 1st credible history of the Mafia ever to be written in Italian was only published after Capaci.

Less than 2 months after Falcone's death, disbelief and indignation swept across Italy once more, when Paolo Borsellino and 5 members of his escort were killed by a massive car bomb outside his mother's house.

Their deaths proved for eternity the existence of a centralised criminal organisation called Cosa Nostra – a secret society that has murder as its very raison d'etre, and has been an integral part of the way Italy has been run since about 1860.

For several months the people of Palermo protested their disgust at the Mafia.

7,000 troops were sent to Sicily to assist the police and release them to hunt for Mafia boss Riina.

It was at this time that the interesting story of Rita Atria emerged.

Rita was born into a Mafia family in Partanna in 1974.

During the Mafia wars in that town (1985-91), about 30 people were killed.

One of these was her father, Vito Atria, who was killed by an opposition Family in 1985.

Vito's son Nicola was also a Mafioso, and he swore to take revenge for his father's killing. In 1991 however, he was killed by Mafia childhood friends. As a result of his murder, his wife Piera Aiello, and then Rita, broke with omerta, and collaborated with both the police and with Paolo Borsellino. They named those who had killed Vito and Nicola.

They also confirmed that the Acardo Family ran the local drugs business, and that it was headed by 3 brothers.

The evidence from Piera and Rita, succeeded in locking up many of the Partanna Mafiosi. Sadly this did not include the Mafioso Vincenzo Calicchia who had been mayor for 30 years.

Because of her collaboration and the breaking of omerta, Rita was rejected by her mother, and by her only sister.

Rita reacted immediately by rejecting her mother, by saying that under no circumstances should her mother attend her funeral – or see her in death.

The death of Falcone, and then of Borsellino two months later, made Rita feel depressed and isolated. She needed Borsellino not only for physical protection, but to give her moral strength.

One week after the death of Borsellino in 1992, Rita Atria threw herself from the 7th floor window of her "safe house" in Rome. She was 18.

Interestingly, her mother went on to destroy her tombstone with a hammer.

Rita was not a pentito because she had nothing to repent.

She was a "witness for justice", a title that became recognised and respected in law in 2001, 9 years after her death.

In 2008, Piera Aiello was nominated as president of the Anti-Mafia association called "Rita Atria".

The film director Marco Amenti made 2 documentaries on Rita's life and death.

After Borsellino's murder and in a display of incredible bravery, a magistrate from Turin, Gian Carlo Caselli, volunteered to take the vacancy left by

Borsellino, and inject new energy into the fight against the mafia.

As a result:

- Dozens of arrests followed.
- A law to protect pentiti was passed.
- Pentiti were given new identities.
- The DIA and DNA were brought on stream.
- The police were given powers to infiltrate the mafia.
- New prison conditions for Mafiosi prevented them from conducting their business from behind bars. They were given solitary confinement.

Coinciding with this drive against Cosa Nostra, there was a general crack down on political corruption throughout Italy.

By the end of 1993, 33% of all Italian MP's were under investigation for corruption, and both the major parties – the DC and the Socialists – had ceased to exist.

Inside Cosa Nostra, things were also changing.

When Riina showed no sign of changing his aggressive tactics after the murders of Falcone and Borsellino, many more Mafiosi turned pentiti.

The legacy of Riina's aggressive strategy was later analysed by many as being a significant cause for the major setback suffered by the Mafia in general, and the Corleonesi in particular. His tactics used to preserve his power base had not only increased the floodtide of pentiti, it had also caused such public anger that the state had no choice but to focus its attentions on suppressing the Mafia.

In January 1993, Riina at the age of 63 (born 1930),was arrested in Palermo by Captain De Caprio as a result of information received from Mafia boss Di Maggio. This help was needed since Riina had been on the run for about 25 years, and the last photo of him dated back to 1969.

The following day, his mentor and Godfather, Luciano Leggio, died of a heart attack in a Sardinian prison at the age of 68.

He had suffered generally from poor health in the form of TB of the spine and more latterly from bladder problems. He had remained unmarried.

At his peak, he was quite a vain man and enjoyed being a snappy dresser. He had very much played to the cameras whenever he had made a court appearance.

He was buried in Corleone.

After Riina's arrest, the leadership of Cosa Nostra passed to his brother-in-law and long term associate, Leoluca Bagarella.

After 20 years of domination by Riina, Cosa Nostra did not respond well to this.

Even Corleonesi diehards like Giovanni Brusca who had played a leading role in the murder of Falcone, found the change unsettling.

What didn't change however was the intention to continue Riina's "massacre" strategy against the state.

The objective was to bring the state to the negotiating table.

They embarked on a bombing campaign in Rome, Florence, and Milan.

Also in 1993, by terrorising the state, the Mafia made an enemy of the Roman Catholic Church.

Ten years earlier, Pope John Paul II had visited Sicily and never mentioned the Mafia, despite the second Mafia war that had raged at that time.

These were now different times and in 1993 even a group of Catholic intellectuals denounced "the scandalous links between representatives of the Catholic Church, and exponents of Mafia power".

Two days later, on a tour of Sicily, Jean Paul II whilst in Agrigento, launched a thundering improvised condemnation of "Mafia culture – a culture of death, profoundly inhuman, anti-evangelical".

Cosa Nostra's response was to bomb 2 churches in Rome. Then they murdered an anti-Mafia priest in Palermo.

In continuing Riina's strategies, the Bagarella faction decided to make an exemplary punishment of a supergrass in order to discourage further pentiti. They identified Mario di Matteo who was part of the Brusca clan.

He had been arrested in June 1993, accused of murder, and had begun to talk in October. He proceeded to implicate Riina, Bagarella and Brusca in Falcone's murder.

As a result, in November 1993, 12 year old Giuseppe di Matteo was kidnapped, and his father who was in a safe house in Italy received a warning to stop talking.

Di Matteo refused to withdraw his evidence and to stop talking despite his son's abduction.

Bagarella's wife, who had been unable to conceive, was made very depressed by Giuseppe's kidnapping. It was thought that this was instrumental in her hanging herself in May 1994.

Although Giuseppe's abduction was conceived by Bagarella, it was performed and managed by Brusca.

In January 1996, after 2 years and 3 months as a hostage, and now aged 14, his emaciated body was strangled to death.

His body was dissolved in acid.

Brusca revealed the details of this barbaric crime after he became a pentito, together with the fact that di Matteo never relented despite knowing the inevitable fate that would befall his son.

In 1996, the number of pentiti peaked at 424. Cosa Nostra was disintegrating despite Riina's tough stance against them.

He had earlier decreed that "we've got to kill them and their relatives to a 20th remove, starting with children of 6 and over".

Armed with the evidence of the pentiti, investigators soon established who had killed Falcone and Borsellino, who had planted the bombs, and who had murdered the priest.

In 1995, Leoluca Bagarella had been arrested in an apartment in Palermo.

In 1996, Giovanni Brusca and his brother Enzo were arrested in Agrigento by Renato Cortese.

One month later, 19 year old Giovanni Riina (son of Toto) who had been groomed by Bagarella in order to consolidate his position, was arrested and later given a life sentence.

Second son, Giuseppe Salvatore Riina (Salvuccio) was later given an 8 year sentence. Both sons had readily followed their father into the Mafia.

It was devastating to Riina's wife Ninetta that both her sons as well as her husband were in prison. Thankfully her two daughters were obviously not eligible to join the Mafia.

By this time Riina's massacre strategy had been abandoned, Cosa Nostra was in crisis, and staring defeat in the eyes.

By the end of 1995, Riina's property fortune of around £125,000,000 had been confiscated, although it is accepted that this was probably not his entire fortune. It was speculated that his fortune was somewhere in the region of £1.3 billion.

His "unlived in", high status Corleone villa was confiscated and then converted into a college.

The unacceptable behaviour of politicians at the time was well illustrated by the 1995 trial of Giulio Andreotti, who was 7 times the DC prime minister of Italy. He was accused of working with the Mafia and using it as an instrument of government.

Lots of unpleasant facts were revealed during the trial, but he was unconvincingly acquitted in 1999.

The "not guilty" verdict was confirmed on appeal in 2003.

He was very much saved by the statute of limitations.

In a separate trial and appeal process, Andreotti was given 24 years in prison for ordering the Mafia to murder a journalist who was blackmailing him in 1979. This judgement was overturned on appeal, and he remains free despite it being established that he definitely had connections with Cosa Nostra until 1981.

After 1995, Cosa Nostra became very low profile.

Italy had been shocked by the violence of the early 90's, but had been placated by the arrests of Riina, Bagarella, and Brusca.

Milan and Rome lost interest in Sicily, but in the silence, Cosa Nostra had begun to restructure, and so Italy let a historic opportunity to defeat the Mafia slip through its fingers.

After the arrest of Bagarella in 1995, Bernardo "the tractor" Provenzano, became the boss of the Corleonesi.

He had been on the run as a fugitive from justice since 1963, and the last photo of him was taken in 1959 when he was 26.

His ability to avoid capture illustrated the power of Mafia territorial control.

He was considered to be more astute than Riina, both in business and in politics.

He was born in 1933 and was 1 of 7 brothers.

He began his career as a debt collector for a loan firm set up by Luciano Leggio, and then to recycling drug money.

He later moved into health, construction, and waste management.

He liked businesses that were dominated by the public sector, so that he could access them via corrupt politicians.

As mentioned earlier, he also had plenty of blood on his hands.

After taking control in 1995 however, Provenzano changed Cosa Nostra strategy. His primary focus was to take it below the radar of public discussion.

His main consiglieri was Lipari.

He believed that "what does not exist in the media, does not exist in reality".

His other priority was to achieve internal peace within Cosa Nostra.

What became known as "pax Mafiosi" was achieved by the following:

- No murders of prominent representatives of the state.
- Murders were restricted to businessmen who were made to die some distance away from the big cities.
- Reducing petty crime around Palermo and Catania.
- A more conciliatory management style, with a greater inclination to profit share.
- He aimed to be centralised, but not as dictatorial as Riina had been.
- He re-established protection rackets as a priority, as beatings and terror could usually achieve this without resorting to murder. The

payment of pizzo (protection money) increased during the Provenzano years.

- He targeted public works contracts, and EU grant money.

There were no longer any heroin refineries in Sicily. This work was now done in the poppy growing countries, but Sicily remained a major point of access to the American market.

The Sicilian Mafia was now coming to accommodations with the emerging criminal organisations of Eastern Europe.

The profits from all these illegal activities became easier to disguise, recycle, move, and invest.

Technical expertise became more available and often the children of Mafiosi were becoming lawyers, bankers and property dealers.

Provenzano's major achievement was to stem the tide of pentiti.

This was done by:

- Instead of killing them, he persuaded them to retract and return to the Family. This was helped by him re-establishing the priority of financially looking after Mafiosi who were in prison.
- Beginning initiations again, but on a very very selective basis. In the main, it was for young men whose families were already steeped in Mafia history.

- Provenzano surrounding himself by older bosses who would take the long term view rather than rash short termism.

In the meantime, the value of pentiti evidence had been questioned by the courts.

As a result:

- The benefits that magistrates could offer them in return for information had been cut.
- Only information provided by the pentiti during their first 6 months would be valid for court use.

It again fell to Renato Cortese to lead the hunt for Provenzano.

He had no direct leads, but pentiti information enabled him to search medical records that painted a more accurate picture of the elusive boss. This was accelerated when Cortese established that Provenzano had his prostate removed in 2003.

The new profile for the 70 year old told the following:

- His prostate was removed which resulted in the use of incontinence pads.
- He was 5 feet 6 inches tall.
- He weighed 10 stones 8 pounds.
- He was a non-smoker and non-drinker.
- He had rheumatism.
- He had a cyst on his right kidney.
- He had false teeth.

They also established that he had 2 sons with his long-term partner Saveria to whom he was not married.

Both of the sons had been kept free from the Mafia by Saveria.

Angelo, the eldest, despite not being in the Mafia, was persecuted when he attempted various legitimate business enterprises.

He was persecuted because of his name.

Paolo, the younger son was a linguist and lived in Germany.

Both sons struggled to come to terms with their father's lifestyle.

From November 2004, it became established that Provenzano had taken refuge in a shack that was a converted sheep pen. It was located about 1 mile away from Corleone, on Horses' Mountain.

Cortese's progress in his search was sabotaged when, early in 2005, the Palermo prosecutors ordered the arrest of 50 of Provenzano's lieutenants. They persuaded themselves that this action would leave Provenzano isolated. From Cortese's perspective, he had lost the very people who he hoped would lead him to his quarry.

The strategy didn't work, and so Cortese had to go back to the drawing board.

In March 2005 he created a team of 24 elite officers who became known as Team Cathedral. They employed the use of high technology to help them with their search.

For their starting point they focussed on the town of Corleone, with particular emphasis on Provenzano's partner Saveria, and their son Angelo, who lived there together.

From the shack, Provenzano continued to rule the Sicilian Mafia, but his authority was beginning to be questioned, because of his age, more fragile state of health, and his very very cautious style of leadership and management.

Cortese and his team had to be extremely furtive in order not to arouse suspicion in Corleone.

They began to watch the shack, but although suspicious, they were never able to observe anyone living there. They saw locals come and go from the farm operation, but never had sight of Provenzano.

They then focussed on the possibility that if he was living there, he would need a laundry service.

By employing the use of bugging devices, high powered cameras and binoculars, they set about trying to prove this.

Their suspicions were further aroused when they found that the electricity use by the building had quadrupled in recent time. There was also use during the night-time hours when nobody appeared to be present.

The laundry service theory turned out to be proved, and although not 100% certain, they eventually rushed the shack, forced an entry, and jubilantly arrested Provenzano.

The inside of the shack was small, scruffy and messy. There was also lots of evidence of his devotion to the Catholic Church.

He was deeply religious, read the bible daily, and had no problem reconciling his religion with his criminal activities.

It was hard to understand why he never ventured outside of the shack, and that he was happy to accept conditions that were worse than most prisons.

It was also hard to understand how he wielded such power when he was old (73), not well, and totally isolated.

With Provenzano, Riina, Riina's eldest son, Bagarella, and Brusca, all in prison, the Corleonesi were finished.

Over a decade, the state confiscated £4.5 billion from Provenzano and his lieutenants.

Provenzano owned nothing, all property was registered in the names of no less than 400 associates.

After Provenzano's arrest in 2006, one of the contenders to fill the power vacuum was the elderly Palermo boss, Salvatore Lo Piccolo (born 1942).

He had initially opposed the Corleonesi, but then jumped on their bandwagon.

He had also forged an alliance with the Mafiosi who had fled from the Corleonesi to America in the early 1980s as a result of the 2nd Mafia war.

Lo Piccolo thought he would be able to call on the alliance to return to Sicily and assist him with his bid for power.

His chances were wrecked in 2007, when he and his son were both arrested.

Three months later, in 2008, in an operation codenamed "Old Bridge", police and FBI agents in America and Italy arrested 77 Mafia suspects, many of whom were alleged allies of Lo Piccolo.

This stifled the return of the American Mafiosi to Sicily.

Another leading candidate to replace Provenzano was Messina Denaro, who was in his 40s (born 1962).

He was a mix of traditional and modernity.

He followed the traditions but lived the life of a millionaire playboy, collecting girlfriends, designer clothes and Rolex watches.

This was a total contrast to Riina and Provenzano who wanted power for power's sake, and who accumulated wealth because it represented power. They had no desire to flaunt their wealth or spend their money on luxurious lifestyles.

The Corleonesi may have been defeated but the battle against the Mafia is far from being won.

Sadly the battle is hardly being fought except by the courageous few.

There is a need to persuade thousands of bar owners, shopkeepers, businessmen and industrialists to stop paying protection money to the Mafia. It is this money that is used to corrupt and to form the shadow state. Roughly 80% of Sicilian businesses pay protection money (pizzo) to Cosa Nostra.

It seems that an overwhelming majority of Sicilians appear to be resigned to the Mafia ruling much of their lives.

Over the years, the Mafia has shown its incredible adaptability and ability to respond to changes around it.

Since it started in 1860, it has survived:

- Capitalism.
- The emergence of the nation state.
- Socialism.
- Fascism.
- Global war.
- Industrialisation.
- The impact of the EU.
- The advance of technology.

The last important political tasks for Provenzano had been to improve things for prisoners like Riina and Bagarella, who were serving long prison sentences, but who had not become pentiti. To avoid division with this faction had been his priority.

What he tried to achieve for them was:

- Reform in prison conditions so that they could run their businesses from jail.
- Changes to the laws of confiscation of Mafia properties.
- Evidence from pentiti to be made invalid.

In 2010 the Mafia continued to be a feared secret society, which acts as a shadow state, and which conducts its business by following the money regardless of whether it's legal or illegal, and regardless of who is in political power.

For the Mafia to die, it is essential that Sicilians must trust the Italian state, more than it fears Cosa Nostra.

Only time will tell whether the Mafia will continue to grow and prosper, or whether it will implode into civil war and self-destruction. Many well informed people predict that it will not only survive, but will continue to succeed.

In 2000, Tomasso Buscetta had died of cancer in America.

He was 72, and died in the belief that the Mafia had won!

POST SCRIPT

It was reported in 2012 that the Mafia was showing its usual pragmatic flexibility by capitalising (literally) on the desperate economic crisis that exists throughout the whole of Italy.

Because of the liquidity problems that businesses are experiencing, the Mafia is stepping in to fulfill the role of the reluctant banks by making loans readily available. The downside to this relief is that they are applying crippling rates of interest which make repayments all but impossible, and hence push enterprises to the wall. They are then taken over by the Mafia because of failed repayments.

Rather than restrict themselves to operations in Sicily, the Mafia has spread to the mainland and has collaborated with the Camorra of Naples, the Ndrangheta of Calabria and the Sacra Unita of Puglia. The combined resource of this organised crime is known as MAFIA INC, and is now regarded as the biggest company and the biggest bank in Italy.

By breaking out of their traditional strongholds, and by collaborating with each other, MAFIA INC is estimated to have a combined resource of:

- An annual turnover of 140 billion euros.
- Cash reserves of 65 billion euros.
- An annual profit of 100 billion euros.

This ramped up loan-sharking business has enabled them to snap up huge numbers of ailing businesses.

It seems that the average mobster is no longer a gun-toting hoodlum but a savvy businessman in a sharp suit with a smart phone and a sophisticated knowledge of finance.

The Mafia's influence in the wealthy north, including Milan the business capital, has been made easier by the "complicity" of some politicians, as well as by professionals such as lawyers and accountants.

It has been said that the new technocrat government of Mario Monti needs to help firms "retake the territory occupied by the Mafia", but that it will be an uphill struggle.

Organised crime now controls everything from gambling to construction and the disposal of industrial and household waste. It has also tightened its grip on the areas of public health, transport and logistics. Gambling is particularly lucrative as this is a 76 billion euro market, and is Italy's third biggest industry.

History continues to illustrate that the Mafia is pretty well impossible to suppress for anything other than a moment in time, or until it has regrouped.

In 2013, anti-Mafia investigators won a court order against Vito Nicasti, a Sicilian businessman who had accumulated great wealth from his involvement in wind farms. They confiscated 1.3 billion euros worth of cash and assets - the biggest haul of Mafia assets ever taken from an individual.

Alternative energy is exactly the kind of business that the Mafia likes to target: awash with cash from state subsidies. It is the perfect place for them to launder their ill-gotten wealth, and win lucrative contracts by the use of bribes. In the wind and solar sectors, all the Mafia needs if it is to get its hands on public money, is the right corrupt political connections.

1900 – 1931
The Mafia in America

Emigration to the USA
Joe Petrosino
Giuseppe "Piddu" Morello
The Volstead Act
The Valachi Papers
Nicola Gentile
The Castellammarese War

Between 1901 and 1913, some 1.1 million Sicilians emigrated – a little less than 25% of the island's population.

Of these, roughly 800,000 made the USA their destination.

Inevitably, some of these were "men of honour", who were smart and ruthless criminals, and who were intent on pursuing their criminal activities on a new and fertile soil.

For most of the 1800's, men on the run in Sicily had sought refuge in the USA. The lemon trade had already connected Palermo with New York.

American police had already connected the Mafia with some violent deaths.

Particularly notable was the murder of New Orleans Police Chief David Hennessy in 1890.

The Sicilian suspects were lynched.

But it was only from the days of the great immigration after 1900, that the traffic between the US and Sicily in criminal ideas, resources, and personnel, became a vital part of Mafia operations.

It is inevitable that mass uncontrolled immigration will encourage the influx of a significant criminal populace.

It is interesting that history has repeated itself 100 years later in England, as a result of mismanaged mass immigration. In this case the criminals have originated from Eastern Europe.

In the early 1900's, America was a tough place to be for the immigrants. It was not so well organised, and personal networks were of paramount importance.

There was also considerable competition and friction with other immigrant communities, who all confined themselves to different ghettos.

Elizabeth Street in Manhattan's Lower East Side was the heart of the New York Sicilian community. In 1905, roughly 8,200 Italians – most of them Sicilians lived there.

It may have been hard, but it was better than Sicily, and represented a new beginning.

It was a chance to better themselves.

This was the dynamic environment into which the Mafia transplanted itself.

As businessmen they could move quickly and flexibly.

With the approval and the assistance of the capo back home, individual Mafiosi could take the Mafia brand anywhere they chose, setting up more or less temporary trading posts as they went.

They were not of course just businessmen, they were also administrators of a shadow state.

A great deal had to be put in place in order for the Mafia system of territorial control through cosche to spread outside of western Sicily.

This included protection rackets, the agreement of neighbouring cosche, a friendly attitude from elements of the press, the police, the judiciary, the local population, and so on.

Exporting this privatised form of government was a slow and painstaking affair.

Even in western Sicily, the extent of the Mafia's domination varied from place to place.

Also it should be noted, that after 150 years of history, the Mafia still has only isolated outposts on the Italian mainland.

The fertile criminal soil of the US was one of the rare environments into which the Mafia method was able to be transported wholesale.

The story of 2 Italian American men – Joe Petrosino and Giuseppe "Piddu" Morello -- brings the Mafia's arrival in America into sharp relief.

Joe Petrosino was born in Salerno in southern Italy in 1860.

He emigrated to America with his parents as a young boy.

He worked hard as a young man and learned to read and write at New York City's public schools.

He took an opportunity to join the New York police where he soon experienced the effects of Mafia crime, and their intimidatory tactics on witnesses.

He was a short but very powerful man.

This was where he met Morello and his gang, all of whom had excellent cover stories for their criminal activities (eg: traders in citrus fruit, oil, cheese, and wine, from Sicily).

All of the Mafiosi found it easy, by methods of corruption, to obtain legal firearms.

A Mafioso could leave Palermo and be confident that he would have a legal firearm soon after clearing through Ellis Island.

Incidentally, in New Orleans in the early 1900's there were about 12,000 Sicilians, and a strong Mafia presence.

The Morello gang based themselves in New York and contained Mafiosi from a number of different cosche from around Palermo.

There were obvious links to the old country, both in personnel and in criminal methods and attitudes.

The main difference was that society in America was much more mobile than the one back in Sicily.

The Mafia needed to be as mobile as the Italian population they preyed on. They initially had little influence outside these communities.

Piddu Morello, who only had only one little finger, was generally seen as the supreme boss of the whole American branch of the Mafia till 1909.

By the time the Morello cosca had set up operations in Manhattan's Little Italy, the New York market place had already been an arena of furious competition for years. There were gangs of different complexions. Some were Italians, some Jewish, some Irish, and some a mixture of all of these.

Against this background the Mafia was able to carve out a competitive slot, but found it impossible to dominate.

As a compliment however, the term 'mafia' became a generic term to describe organised crime, much as 'hoover' is used to describe a vacuum cleaner.

"The Black Hand" (Mano Nera) was also a term used in the violence industry before the Mafia emerged, and may have been a precursor.

Black Hand blackmail letters became a criminal fashion which would never have been tolerated in Sicily, where they brutally protected their monopoly of territorial intimidation.

Joe Petrosino's reputation continued to grow as a good honest cop, and he was seen as a new kind of hero to many New Yorkers.

In 1905, he was appointed head of the force's new Italian Branch, and he was responsible for sending hundreds of Italians back to Europe.

He also imprisoned many.

He was the first Italian American to make lieutenant and in 1907 married an Italian girl in Little Italy.

In 1908, he was awarded a gold watch by the Italian government for his part in the arrest of a leading Neapolitan gangster.

In 1909, Petrosinno became head of a new secret service arm of the police department.

His first mission was to return to Italy to set up an independent information network on gangsters with criminal records in Sicily. His hope was to block them at the point of immigration.

He was a vulnerable target and was killed by the Mafia in Palermo whilst in the process of collecting this information.

When his body was returned to New York, an estimated 20,000 people came to pay their respects.

No-one was charged with the murder and the case remained unsolved.

Not long after Petrosino's death in 1909, Piddu Morello was given 25 years in prison for counterfeiting. Because of this, he lost his role as head of the organisation.

In 1919, the landscape of organised crime in America altered radically.

The greatest stimulation that the Mafia has ever received was the implementation of the Volstead Act, which provided for the enforcement of the 18th Amendment.

This act was not abolished until 1933. This was the period known as Prohibition.

It meant that the manufacture, sale and transportation of intoxicating liquor was banned.

We now know that whenever a substance or service is banned by law, it creates a market vacuum that is immediately satisfied by organised crime.

At a stroke, Prohibition gave an estimated $2 billion into the illegal economy during its 14 year existence.

Prohibition was the result of the successful lobbying of the Temperance League and the Anti-German Brewers lobby (World War I had just finished).

At the same time, the public resented the Volstead Act, and so the gangsters became the consumer's friend.

The illegal suppliers became known as bootleggers, and stills were used to produce the illegal moonshine that was often of a very rough quality.

The vast profits from booze, and the public's benign attitude to its illegal manufacture, also lowered the threshold for corruption.

Police, politicians, and the judiciary all took their share of the bonanza by means of the bribes they received.

The Mafia were not the dominant players during Prohibition.

In the New York area, 50% of bootleggers were Jewish compared with about 25% who were Italian.

Much later, in 1963, Joe Valachi, an American Mafioso who thought he was going to be killed in prison by the Mafia, decided to turn pentito. Valachi was a hit man for the Genovese crime Family.

He confessed to the Congressional Sub-Committee on organised crime which included Robert Kennedy.

Kennedy described Valachi's evidence as the biggest single intelligence breakthrough in combating organised crime.

The Valachi Papers were a sensation, although to put it in perspective, he was only a low ranking soldier who would have had limited information or dealings with the bosses.

He confirmed the use of the name Cosa Nostra, and described Mafia life in the 20's and 30's, including the Castellammarese War of 1930/31. He also detailed the murder of Maranzano, to whom he had been a chauffeur.

The Valachi Papers were published in 1968 and were a collaboration between Valachi and the author Peter Maas. The book was made into a film in 1972, one year after Valachi died in prison of a heart attack.

Better information regarding the American Mafia in the 1920's and 30's came from Nicola Gentile, a man born in Sicily but initiated in Philadelphia in 1905.

He was known as Nick or Cola depending on which side of the Atlantic he found himself.

In 1963, at almost 80 years, and in retirement in Rome where he died in poverty, Gentile decided to write an autobiography via a journalist.

He was the first Mafioso to tell his story this way.

He was an embittered old man whose children had established themselves in professional careers, but were ashamed of their criminal family background.

They had shunned the man who had paid for their educations and houses.

Gentile had worked with the most famous bosses of the 1920's and 30's. These included:

- Joe "the boss" Masseria.
- Al Capone.
- Lucky Luciano.
- Vincenzo Mangano.
- Albert Anastasia.
- Vito Genovese.

Surprisingly Cola Gentile's Italian testimony remains untranslated and unknown to all but a few people outside of Italy.

Interestingly in New York's docks in the 1880's, 95% of the city's longshoremen were Irish. By 1919, 75% were Italian.

This became fertile ground for the Mafia. There was a ruthless protection regime in the docks, provided by Albert Anastasia and Vincent Mangano.

Gentile had been born near Agrigento in Sicily.

He arrived in America in 1903 at the age of 18. He was a tough youth, and was classic Mafioso material.

He started as a salesman in Kansas City, but was initiated in Philadelphia.

After 3 years, he returned to Sicily, to marry and have a child.

In 1915, he went to Pittsburgh where he brutally rose to become the crime boss by totally dominating other Italian criminal factions.

He also later operated in San Francisco and Brooklyn.

New York's position within the American Mafia operation was always dominant, and it always provided the "Capo dei Capi" (boss of bosses). This situation was similar to the Sicilian Mafia being dominated by Palermo.

Gentile developed a reputation for being a roving mediator. This is possibly why he travelled so much around America, as opposed to controlling a territorial cosca.

He related how Joe "the Boss" Masseria came to power in 1928 after Frankie Yale (real name Ioele) was assassinated in Brooklyn by Capone for cheating him over alcohol shipments. He also painted a picture of

Charles "Lucky" Luciano, who left Sicily at the age of 9.

Their rise coincided with the Americanisation of the Mafia.

Al Capone was born in Brooklyn of Neapolitan parents. He eventually moved to Chicago as a gunman and rose to the top of the Chicago underworld in the mid 1920's.

His syndicate included non-Italians.

Capone's womanising and greed for publicity would have been very much frowned on in Sicily.

The St. Valentine's Day massacre in 1929 was attributed to Capone.

It was people like Capone and Luciano, by having strong ties outside the Sicilian and Italian communities, who accelerated the Americanisation process within the Mafia, as Prohibition came to a close.

Some of the Jewish and Irish gangs were equally as brutal and dominant as the Mafia, but due to a lack of tradition they have not had the longevity.

It also came from Gentile that the Palermo Mafiosi tended to stay in Sicily, and that it was those from smaller towns like Agrigento, or tiny coastal towns like Castellammare, who would emigrate for better career opportunities within the Mafia.

Gentile described the Castellammarese war of 1930-31, so called because the Mafiosi of one side largely came from Castellammare del Golfo.

They were led by Salvatore Maranzano, who arrived in New York in 1927 as a refuge from fascism in Sicily.

His opponent, Joe "the Boss" Masseria, who was considered to be "the Boss of Bosses", came from Palermo.

One of the first of the many Mafiosi victims of this war was Piddu Morello.

Maranzano accused Masseria of being too dictatorial, and accused him of losing the confidence of his soldiers.

He also criticised him for admitting Al Capone (a non-Sicilian, stained by pimping) into the Mafia.

In April 1931, Joe "the Boss" was having lunch with one of his lieutenants, Lucky Luciano.

They began to play cards, but when Luciano went to the toilet, the hit man he had hired entered the room and shot Masseria dead.

Having removed his own Boss, Luciano then sought peace terms with Maranzano.

As a result Maranzano became "Capo dei Capi".

In September 1931, the newly crowned Boss became deeply unpopular and untrusted which resulted in him being stabbed and shot to death by hitmen, again employed by Lucky Luciano.

The Castellammarese war was over, ended by the murder of both its leading combatants. These murders were both orchestrated by Luciano, who had placed himself into the most dominant position within Cosa Nostra.

Luciano also had big connections with criminals from other ethnic groups, notably Jewish and Irish.

Maranzano's death can be taken as marking a point when the Mafia in America became an Italian-American organisation, rather than a Sicilian one. Luciano was the dominant player at the dawn of this new era.

As the American version absorbed non-Sicilians from Italy, the two organisations gradually separated, although certain links survived.

Having said that, the core of American Mafia membership remained ethnically Sicilian after 1931.

In Buffalo, Stefano Magaddino, from Sicily, was Boss from the 1920's till his death in 1974.

The American brand would always need to employ Sicilian principles if it was to both survive and succeed.

1931 – 2011
The American Mafia

The Five Families
The hierarchy
The Chicago Syndicate
Apalachin
The RICO Act
The Mafia Commission Trial
The Pizza Connection Trial
Rudy Giuliani
The new millennium

This book is primarily about the Sicilian Mafia, but because it gave birth to the American version, it seems appropriate to give a brief summary of the development of this muscular offspring.

The last chapter mentioned how immigration in the late 1800s and the early 1900s was the means by which the Mafia seed was planted in America.

Also covered was the Prohibition era, the rise of Joe Masseria, and the Castellammarese War in New York which left Salvatore Maranzano as the capo dei capi.

During his 6 months in this supreme position, and before he was murdered in September 1931, Maranzano divided New York into 5 territorial Families. Each had a boss and under boss.

- Gagliano + Luchese, which later became the Luchese Family.
- Luciano + Genovese, which later became the Genovese Family.
- Profaci + Magliocco, which later became the Colombo Family.
- Mangano Bros + Anastasia, which later became the Gambino Family.
- Bonanno + Galente, which later became the Bonanno Family.

For most of the 20th century, there were 26 cities around the USA that had Cosa Nostra Families, but as Palermo had dominated Sicily, so New York dominated the USA. As a rough estimate, it is considered that this incredibly corrosive influence by the Mafia in America was effected by a mere 3-4,000 Mafiosi.

The American Mafia began with a strict hierarchical structure which was basically the same as the Sicilian version and was introduced by Salvatore Maranzano in 1931.

By using this chain of command, the higher levels of the organisation are insulated from incrimination if a lower level member should be captured by law enforcement.

The levels are as follows:

- Boss --- the boss is the head of the family and makes all final decisions. He is sometimes referred to as the Don or Godfather. He may be elected by the caporegimes, or he may use force of personality to make a "power grab". In the case of a tied vote, the underboss would cast a deciding vote. The boss takes a cut of every operation undertaken by every member of the Family.

- Underboss --- the underboss is usually appointed by the boss and is the second in command of the Family. He is in charge of all the capos in the Family, and is usually first in line to become acting boss if the boss is imprisoned, unless the Don names an alternative successor.

- Consigliere --- this is a position of great trust that is chosen by the boss, to advise him and to mediate on his behalf. This role was traditionally played by more senior individuals.

- Caporegime (or capo) --- this position is like a captain or skipper who is in charge of a crew of 10-20 soldiers and many more associates, who report directly to him. The capo is chosen by the boss, to whom he gives a percentage of the crew's earnings. He is also responsible for any murders that are assigned to him. The capo, who has considerable power, will be closely monitored by the boss and underboss, to make sure that he doesn't cheat the system.

- Soldier --- This is an initiated Mafioso who is part of the Family, and needs to have Italian ancestry, preferably on his father's side. He will be totally obedient to his superiors and will have already murdered (made his bones) on their instructions. He will follow the rules and the orders of the Mafia without question, and the fact that he has murdered makes him totally reliable. Also known as a "man of honour" or "made man", his initiation is the same as that described in a previous chapter.

- Associate --- These are not part of the family, but act as errand boys or as outsourced services, which keep the heat off Family members. They may be corrupt union officials or businessmen. Non-Italians will never rise above this rank, but Italians are effectively auditioned at this level in order to establish their suitability for initiation into Cosa Nostra membership. Initiations do not occur on a random basis, and only happen every 5-10 years as agreed by the Mafia Commission, with the objective of renewing and replenishing numbers.

The American Mafia had to be much more adaptable than its parent, if for no other reason than the fact that Sicilians were in such a small minority in such a huge and populous country.

It was for these reasons that the Sicilians worked with other Italian criminal groups, and were happy to initiate them into the Mafia if they were thought to be suitable.

From starting as the Sicilian Mafia, it became a pan-Italian Mafia, and then an Italian American organisation, as subsequent generations of American born men with Italian ancestry became initiated.

The most prominent American Mafiosi can be seen by studying the family trees of the 5 New York Families that were created by Maranzano in 1931.

The Gambino Family:

- 1931-51. This started with Vincent Mangano as boss and Anastasia as underboss. Anastasia was also the boss of Murder Incorporated. He was known as The Lord High Executioner. After 20 years he eventually whacked Mangano in 1951 and thereby became the new boss.
- Albert Anastasia was boss from 1951-57, and had Carlo Gambino as his underboss. Anastasia was duly whacked whilst in a barber's chair in New York. The murder was implemented by Gambino at the request of Genovese, although the actual execution was carried out by the Gallo brothers from the Joe Profaci Family.
- Carlo Gambino ruled as boss from 1957-76 when he died of natural causes. He expanded the Family and became not only the boss of bosses but also the most powerful boss in Mafia history. His mild manner, as seen on newsreel footage, totally conccaled the ruthlessness that helped to create his unchallenged power. His underboss was Neil Dellacroce.
- Paul Castellano who ruled from 1976-85 was Gambino's brother-in-law. Dellacroce continued as his underboss. When Dellacroce died of cancer, John Gotti's leadership ambitions became ignited. Castellano's family

came from Brooklyn but after he became boss of the Gambino Family, he later built a multi-million dollar mansion in Todt Hill on Staten Island, which became known as The White House. He was urbane and articulate and assumed the persona of a suited businessman. He also loved the construction industry and it was here that he preferred to focus his criminal activities. Death was the Family's official position on drug dealing, and Castellano repeatedly warned them "Deal in drugs, you die!" As time went by, he became quite reclusive and totally disconnected from his soldiers. The Family then began to lose confidence in him because he began to make a number of decisions that were not judged to be in the Family's interest. Castellano and his loyal aide Tommy Bilotti were whacked outside Sparks Steak House in mid-Manhattan in 1985 on the orders of John Gotti who was heavily involved in drug dealing, and who therefore feared possible retribution from his Boss. As this hit was not authorised by the Commission, it took Cosa Nostra into unchartered territory. Also, because Gotti could not afford for this high profile job to be botched, it was surprising that of the 4 gunmen used for the execution, only 1 was a soldier whilst the other 3 were associates. Castellano had 3 sons, none of whom were initiated into Cosa Nostra.

- 1986-2002. John Gotti became the most publicised boss since Al Capone. Known as the

"Dapper Don", he modelled himself on the Hollywood image of a Mafia boss. He wore $2,000 suits, sported a pinky ring, dined in elegant night-spots and basked in the attention of the media. He based himself at The Ravenight Social Club in Manhattan's Little Italy. His appointed underboss was Sammy "the bull" Gravano, who later testified against Gotti. As the most powerful mobster in New York he even featured on the cover of Time magazine. But his bravado proved his undoing: he was successfully bugged by the FBI, and in court, prosecutors played tapes of his narcissistic rants. He even boasted of killing one underling because "he didn't come when I called". Gotti was born in 1940, the 5th of 13 children, and grew up in a tenement in the Bronx. His father, the son of Neapolitan immigrants, was a hopeless gambler who couldn't hold down a job. Strangely, John also became a degenerate gambler as he rose through the Mafia ranks. At 12, John Gotti began running errands for hoodlums. He then left school at 16 and joined a gang. Having discovered that he had a talent for leg-breaking and lorry-jacking, he started to serve as a mob associate. In 1973, he murdered 2 men at the request of Carlo Gambino – for which he served 2 years. As reward, he was made a capo and given command of the Gambino Family's Bergin crew. Greedy and ambitious, Gotti began to plan his rise within the Gambinos. In 1985 he decided to take control of the Family.

On December 16th 4 heavies in matching raincoats accosted Paul Castellano outside Sparks restaurant in Manhattan, and pumped 6 bullets into his head. Gotti and Gravano were parked nearby, directing the action by walkie-talkie. Afterward, they cruised brazenly past the scene to make sure that Castellano was dead. Days later, Gotti was anointed king of the Gambinos, the most powerful of New York's 5 Families, with 300 members and an annual turnover of $500m. He was also known as the Teflon Don because nothing would "stick" when he was in court. By giving generously to the community he tried to create a lovable image. But there was nothing lovable about Gotti. In 1980, a neighbour accidently ran over and killed Gotti's 12 year old son. Although exonerated from blame, the man disappeared soon after, never to be seen again. Following 3 trial acquittals, Gotti was eventually convicted in 1992 on racketeering and murder charges, including Castellano's. This conviction was very much due to the evidence given by Gravano who was disgusted by the lies told by Gotti during the bugged FBI tapes. These lies, together with his increasing egomania, meant that Gotti was morphing a variant of Cosa Nostra that Gravano could neither accept nor relate to. He was sentenced to life without parole, but died of throat cancer in prison in 2002 at the age of 61. He was buried in St John's Cemetery in Queens along with other famous Mafiosi (Salvatore Maranzano, Carlo

Gambino, Joe Profaci, Joe Colombo, Lucky Luciano, Vito Genovese, Neil Dellacroce, Carmine Galante, Philip Rastelli). Whilst in prison, he retained his celebrity and had received hundreds of fan letters each year. In retrospect however, Gotti made a great gangster, but a lousy crime boss. His attraction to the limelight turned him and his associates into targets, and his taunting of the authorities only spurred them on to catch him. This was the sort of behaviour which provoked the angry criticisms from Joe Bonanno. Gravano observed that everybody has an ego, some have large egos, and then there are those like Gotti who are egomaniacs. Gotti's last mistake was to appoint his notoriously stupid son to succeed him. John Jr. had the mentality of a small time hood and was clearly not up to the job.

- 2002-2003. Peter Gotti (John's older brother) ran the family until he was found guilty of racketeering in 2003 and given a 9 year sentence. In 2004, he was found guilty of conspiring to kill Sammy "the bull" Gravano. This faced a life sentence.
- 2005. Arnold Squitieri became acting boss.
- During the Gambino and Castellano reigns, this Family became the biggest and most powerful in America. After Gotti however, the Gambino Family became a shadow of its former self. The Teflon Don had inflicted more damage on the Mafia in a few years than US enforcement over 5 decades! It is an interesting observation that neither Paul Castellano, Vincent Gigante nor

Sammy Gravano, wanted their sons initiated into the Mafia, whereas Gotti was bursting with pride when his son was "made".

The Bonanno Family.

- Salvatore Maranzano was the first boss and has already been mentioned. He was murdered in 1931.
- 1931-1964. Joe Bonanno (Joe Bannanas) took over and had a long reign. He was an original Commission member and initially ran his Family well. He had arrived in the US from Sicily in 1908 at the age of 3, and began building his criminal empire in Brooklyn during Prohibition. At the age of 26 he became New York's youngest Don and went on to become one of the most powerful figures in the history of the American Mafia. Whilst many of the mobsters flaunted their wealth, Bonanno led a relatively quiet life. His only extravagances were heavily-jewelled rings and expensive cigars. He had always worked to keep the Mafia as Sicilian as possible and had rebuked other mob leaders for accepting non-Sicilians who did not understand the rules of loyalty and deference. He was however forced to retire to Arizona by the Commission after a failed plot to kill other Mafia bosses (Carlo Gambino and Thomas Lucchese), so that he could become the boss of bosses. He had become a dangerous loose cannon.

- 1964-1975. This was a period of internal battles for control of the Family. One of the contenders was Bill Bonanno but none of them were proved to be capable. Joe initially threatened to make a comeback to regain the leadership, but attempts on his life, sanctioned by the Commission, eventually dissuaded him. Looking back on the fate of so many Mafia bosses, it's remarkable that he died peacefully at home in 2002, surrounded by his relatives, at the grand age of 97.
- 1975-1979. Carmine Galante who had been the under boss to Bonanno, schemed during his 20 year jail term to fill the power vacuum and to become the Godfather. On his release from jail, he became the acting boss as a result of his excessive violence. He expanded his huge narcotic trade, and imported Sicilian mobsters, known as zips, to protect him and to bolster his faction. He was regarded as a homicidal predator, and was both feared and hated. He was killed in 1979 on the orders of the Commission, because of his greed and to stop him becoming too powerful. His funeral was only attended by his immediate family. He was shunned in death by the Mafia.
- 1980-1991. Philip Rastelli spent most of his reign in prison on racketeering convictions, where he died of cancer. His underboss was Joseph Massino.
- 1991-2003. Joseph Massino rebuilt the organisation to become the nation's top mob Family, and changed its name to honour

himself. He was convicted on RICO charges in 2004, and became the first New York boss to co-operate with the government. He is serving "life" for 8 murders, but hopes to reduce his sentence by becoming a prosecution witness. This left the future leadership unclear.

The Colombo Family.

- 1931-1962. Joe Profaci was the first boss, along with Joe Magliocco as his underboss. He was also a Commission member. Towards the end of his reign, and before he died of cancer in 1962, he was plagued by a young internal rebellion which was led by Joe Gallo. Magliocco was not acceptable to the Commission and in any event died in 1963.
- 1963-1971. Joseph Colombo was appointed boss, mainly through the support of Carlo Gambino who wanted to manipulate him. With Gambino's help Colombo made his Family strong and wealthy again. He developed a reputation for being a snappy dresser and high roller (totally unlike Carlo Gambino who kept a low and humble profile, despite his incredible power). His tenure was cut short when he was shot and paralyzed in 1971. He was at a protest rally which was demonstrating against prejudice by law enforcement agencies against all Italian Americans. He tried to act as a civil rights leader for the Italian American community but was criticised by the mob for

seeking celebrity status. The shooting, which may have been ordered by the mob, reduced him to a vegetative state. Colombo had become the signature name for the Family.

- 1972-1986. Carmine Persico took firm control until he was convicted in the Commission case and another rackets trial in 1986.
- 1987-Present. Although sentenced to life without parole, Persico tried to maintain control from prison until his son Alphonse was ready to succeed him. This attempt to create a mob dynasty provoked an internal war. Alphonse was convicted of racketeering in 2001, creating a power vacuum and a fractured Family. He was further indicted in 2004 on new charges of murder.
- In July 2010, 93 year old Mafioso John Franzese was convicted after his son testified against him. He was described as an ex-boss of the Colombo Family, and is one of the last survivors of an era when mobsters partied with the likes of Frank Sinatra. Franzese faces up to 20 years in jail for extorting money from 2 strip clubs and a pizzeria. He seemed indifferent about the prospect of dying behind bars.

The Genovese Family.

- Giuseppe (Piddu) Morello was the boss of the Morello Family, which was later called the Genovese Family. He was the first boss of bosses in America.

- He was succeeded by Joe "the boss" Masseria whose murder was related in the previous chapter.
- 1931-1937. Charles "Lucky" Luciano became the boss. After orchestrating the deaths of Masseria and Maranzano, he was concerned about reprisals from the other old time Sicilian Mafiosi from across the country, and so he made a pre-emptive strike to remove about 50 of them within 24 hours. This was known as the night of the Sicilian Vespers. Rather than take the title Capo dei Capi, he founded and chaired the Mafia Commission whose brief it was to arbitrate on interfamily disputes. By introducing the Commission, each boss had an equal say and vote on important matters. He then went on to work out a formula for co-existence with non-Italian organised crime in New York. Hence Luciano was the inspiration for Murder Incorporated which was led by Louis "Lepke" Buchalter who was a dominant force in the city's Garment Centre rackets. Also involved were people such as Meyer Lansky, Benjamin "Bugsy" Siegel, Albert Anastasia, Arthur "Dutch Schultz" Flegenheimer, Allie Tannenbaum, Myer Sycoff, Sholem Bernstein, Mendy Weiss, Harry Teitelbaum, Harry Greenburg and Abe "Kid Twist" Reles. Because of its significant Jewish content, it became known as Kosher Nostra. Murder Incorporated responded to calls from every corner of the country to perform its services and lasted for about 10 years. It is estimated

that it carried out about 1,000 contract killings. Dutch Schultz was whacked on Luciano's instructions for attempting to take unilateral action to murder prosecutor Thomas Dewey. He had been clearly told by the Commission that this murder would have caused too many problems for the mob by the authorities. Bugsy Siegel was made one of Luciano's chief lieutenants, and was sent to develop Hollywood and Las Vegas where he personally opened the Flamingo Hotel as a casino. This creation involved Siegel embarking on an obsessive spending spree for which the mob would never forgive him. The Flamingo project was hopelessly over budget and its opening was a fiasco. The mob felt they were being deceived and ran out of patience. He was duly whacked by being shot in the head. The character of Moe Greene in "The Godfather" was based on Siegel. Meyer Lansky was better known as a financial genius and laundering genius. By 1935, Luciano was the biggest Mob leader the USA had ever known, and had far exceeded Capone. His HQ was the top floors of the Waldorf Astoria where he signed in as Charles Ross. Amongst other things he controlled Tammany Hall which was an infamous political clubhouse that in turn controlled City Hall. Another development was that the Family now had associates working for it that included all nationalities and ethnic groups. These people of course would never be initiated as "made men". Luciano was very big in prostitution and viciously controlled about 200 madams and 1,000 prostitutes. Because of this he was pursued by Thomas E Dewey, the New York special prosecutor. He was convicted of being a prostitution overlord in 1937, and given a sentence of 30 years. His sentence was commuted and he was deported for life to Italy in 1946 where he lived and died of natural causes in 1962 in Naples. It has been suggested that his sentence had been commuted as repayment for the essential and helpful information that he gave to the American armed forces, which helped ease the Allied invasion of Sicily in 1943. This version of events is refuted by many historians.

- 1937-1957. Frank Costello succeeded Luciano, having previously been his consiglieri. This was because Luciano's under boss, Vito Genovese had fled to Sicily as a result of Dewey pursuing him with a murder charge. During Costello's early days as boss, Brooklyn District Attorney William O'Dwyer managed to send Buchalter and several others from Murder Incorporated to the electric chair. Also at this time, Bugsy Siegel was thought to be cheating the syndicate, and was duly executed. Costello hastily retired in 1957 however, after a bullet grazed his head in an assassination attempt which was ordered by his rival Vito Genovese. He had lost much of his authority with the mob as a result of his very weak TV interviews at the Kefauver Hearings. It was this that gave momentum to Genovese's bid to become boss of the Family. Costello had been a virtuoso corruptor, but despite being in charge, both Luciano and Genovese continued to have an input into the Family's affairs. New York mayor Fiorello La Guardia resisted his corrupting influence and proceeded to instigate a purge to successfully drive out Costello's illegal fruit machines. The law enforcement agencies also targeted him for tax evasion. The leading defence lawyer for the most notorious gangsters of the time ---- Costello, Schultz, Luciano, Anastasia, Torrio and Genovese, was George Wolf. Luciano had also used Moses A. Polakoff.

- 1957-1969. Vito Genovese – "Don Vito" – replaced Costello and was back as head of the Luciano Family, as he was in the early 30s. The Family took his name. He believed that Anastasia was encouraging Costello to resume as head of the Family, which is why he encouraged Gambino to organise the murder of Albert Anastasia. He then instigated the fateful meeting of the Commission at Apalachin in order to explain the unauthorised hit on Anastasia. Don Vito was convicted of narcotics trafficking in 1959, but stayed in charge till he died in prison in 1969. Genovese's motto was: "Always kill a brother for revenge". During his acrimonious divorce from his wife Anna, Genovese had her long-time lover whacked.

- 1970-1980s. Philip Lombardo replaced Genovese, but retired in the 1980s because of failing health. He used Anthony Salerno to pose as boss, to deflect attention and deceive law enforcement.

- 1982-Present. Then came Vincent "the chin" Gigante who also used Salerno as a "front" boss, until the latter was sentenced to life in 1986. Gigante faked mental illness for decades until convicted of racketeering in 1997 and 2003. He will not be released from prison, where he still has the title of boss, until 2012 when he will be 84.

The Lucchese Family.

- 1931-1951. Gaetano Gagliano from the Bronx was the first boss of this Family. He kept a low profile and retired with a fatal illness in 1951. His underboss was Gaetano (Thomas) Lucchese.
- 1951-1967. Thomas Lucchese took over and ruled without opposition until he died of cancer in 1967. The Family was named after him.
- 1970- 1986. Antonio "Ducks" Corallo became boss on his release from prison. He was a powerful and effective Godfather until he was convicted in the Commission case trial in 1986.
- 1986-Present. Vittorio Amuso was appointed boss with Anthony Casso as his underboss. Their bloody purge on suspected internal enemies produced numerous defections and convictions. Amuso was given life in 1992, and Casso was given life in 1998 for racketeering

and multiple murder charges. Amuso remained as nominal boss.

The Chicago Mafia.

Chicago has always had a very strong mafia presence as can be shown by looking at the successions within its Family tree.

- 1910-1920. Big Jim Colosimo was executed in 1920 just after the beginning of Prohibition. This was probably organised by Torrio.
- 1920-1925. Johnny Torrio became the Prohibition era boss of the Chicago outfit. He was ex-Brooklyn and returned there in voluntary exile after he handed control to Alphonse Capone.
- 1925-1931. Alphonse Capone (Scarface) was born in 1899 in Brooklyn where he was originally a hit man before moving to Chicago, where he replaced Torrio as boss. The St Valentine's Massacre in 1929 helped Capone achieve criminal dominance. He had used fake police officers to organise the massacre of 7 of the top people in the George Bugs Moran's Irish gang. They had already disposed of Dean (Dion) O'Banion. By 1929, and at the age of 30, he had become the biggest Don in the USA. It is estimated that he had 500 soldiers in the 1920s. The FBI launched University of Illinois graduate Elliot Ness during this period, to smash his syndicate. Ness was incorruptible

and was a serious thorn in the side for the syndicate. By 1930 Capone was then acting as a public benefactor by opening up soup kitchens for the unemployed. It was around this time that he gained further notoriety by killing 2 of his cheating enforcers with a baseball club whilst holding a dinner in their honour. In 1931 however, at the age of 32 he was jailed for 8 years in Alcatraz for tax evasion. This was the only thing for which they could prove him guilty, and was the result of the dedicated work of Arthur P. Madden of the IRS. The jail term turned Capone into a mental wreck. On release in 1939 he was treated for syphilis and retired to Florida where in 1947 at the age of 48, he died of the disease.

- 1931-1943. Frank Nitti succeeded Capone. He had previously been an enforcer for Capone and finished up committing suicide rather than face jail. This was a strange decision since most Mafiosi avoided jail by using intimidation or murder on the relevant witnesses. Ricca had always played a prominent and dominant role during this period.

- 1943-1947. Paul Ricca who had been underboss to Nitti, succeeded him. He survived jail and became an adviser (consiglieri) to both Accardo and Giancana. He was hugely influential in the outfit until his natural death in 1972.

- 1947-1956. Tony Accardo, became the boss of the Chicago Outfit. He had been an ex-minder and enforcer for Capone. He was also suspected of involvement in the St. Valentine's Day Massacre. He was a very powerful personality and lived opulently in a 22 roomed mansion. He retired in favour of Giancana, but like Ricca, retained considerable influence until he died in 1992. No major business or hits were implemented without their consent.

- Sam Giancana, was boss from 1957-1966. As a young hoodlum he had been arrested and rearrested for 3 murder investigations before he was 20. He was also arrested over 60 times for various charges during his criminal career. He was thought to have been involved in a CIA plot to murder Fidel Castro. This is plausible, because Castro had ruined the gambling haven of Havana that had existed during the Batista regime. Antoinette Giancana (Sam's daughter), claimed that John F Kennedy and her father shared the same mistress (Judith Exner). Exner confirmed this. She had been introduced to Giancana by Frank Sinatra who was friendly with both men and who often acted as a go-between. It was also said that Giancana helped get Kennedy elected in Chicago during his presidential campaign by making a huge financial contribution to the Democrats. The boss had hoped that JFK would respond by taking the heat off of his criminal activities. This didn't happen, as Robert Kennedy was made Attorney General and pursued them even more vigorously. Giancana also had a long affair with the famous singer Phyllis McGuire despite her also being said to have a relationship with JFK during part of this time. Giancana was also said to be in partnership with Frank Sinatra at the Cal-Neva lodge on Lake Tahoe, Nevada. Sinatra's name was shown on the deeds of ownership, but in all probability he was also fronting for the Mafia. Giancana had a very powerful control over many of the Las Vegas casinos. This was achieved by a combination of part ownership, intimidation and murder. He was very big into gambling, but also had powerful influence in the movie, record, and juke box industries. Thus he became well connected to many of the stars of the day. Giancana's profile then became criticised by the mob for being too high, and resentment increased because he didn't share enough of his global off-shore gambling spoils (floating casinos). In addition he was on the receiving end of a massive FBI surveillance exercise that was designed to put psychological pressure on him and cause a rift between him and his mob associates. As a result he was deposed by Tony Accardo. He retired into exile in Mexico for about 7 years, but was eventually returned to the US by the Mexican authorities. He was then scheduled to appear before a federal grand jury investigating organised crime. There was concern in the mob that he might enter the witness protection program in order to save himself. As a result, and despite protection, he was shot dead in his home in 1975. His executioner shot him once in the back of the head, before turning him to fire

6 times into his face and neck. This hit was thought to be authorised by Joey Aiuppa. Reading the transcripts of the FBI bugging tapes revealed Giancana to have had a disappointingly limited vocabulary and ability to express himself.

- 1967-1969. Jackie Cerone. He was a former chauffeur to Tony Accardo before he became the boss.
- 1971-1986. Joey Aiuppa. He had earlier been an enforcer for Capone, and then No. 2 to Accardo, before he became boss.
- 1993-Present. John Di Fronzo is reported in Wikipedia as the current boss.

Other prominent Mafiosi in America were:

- Santo Trafficante who was the boss of Florida and who operated in Cuba during the Batista era. He was also thought to be part of the "Castro plot".
- Carlos Marcello who was the boss of New Orleans was also implicated in the plot against Castro.
- Frank Desimone who was boss of L.A.

When Prohibition ended in 1933, alcohol became legal again, and so the Mafia needed to focus on other areas of business.

The Great Depression had started, but the Mafia had become hugely wealthy and had developed its corruption network.

Areas for attention included:

- Illegal gambling.
- Loan sharking.
- Extortion.
- Protection rackets.
- Drug trafficking.
- Fencing.
- Bid rigging and labour racketeering via the unions.
- Prostitution.
- Arms dealing.
- Tax fraud.
- Stock manipulation schemes.
- Waste management.

In the 1950s the Mafia began to control quite a few unions, including the powerful Teamsters. Jimmy Hoffa was the high profile leader of this union. He was very corrupt and used union funds for investments in numerous shady high risk Mafia projects, as well as skimming vast amounts for his own personal use. All this was done at the expense of the rank and file union members. He served a jail term for his illegal activities, but in 1971 obtained an early release from President Richard Nixon with whom he had an enigmatic relationship. Soon after his release, he disappeared and was never seen again. He was presumed murdered by the mob.

After Hoffa's imprisonment, the leadership of the Teamsters passed to Allen Dorfman who was completely controlled by the Mafia who were very possessive about this valuable "cash cow". Because Dorfman knew too much about the Mafia's finances, and could therefore incriminate them, they arranged for him to be whacked in 1983.

Control of the unions allowed the Mafia to make profitable forays into legitimate businesses such as construction, demolition, waste management, trucking, the garment industry and in the waterfront.

In New York, most construction projects couldn't be performed without the Five Families approval.

Operating in the shadows, the Mafia faced little law enforcement, from a body that was either corruptible or ignorant of its existence.

1951 saw the televised Kefauver Hearings as mentioned in a previous chapter. These caused a sensation.

In 1957, the New York State Police uncovered a meeting of major American Cosa Nostra figures from around the country, in a small upstate New York town of Apalachin. This gathering has become known as the Apalachin Meeting. It had been convened in November 1957 after the murder of Albert Anastasia in a Manhattan barber's shop in the October. Many of the attendees were arrested, and this event was the catalyst that changed the way law enforcement battled organized crime.

The establishment of the US Organised Crime Strike Force facilitated efforts to prosecute members of the Mafia. The Strike Force was established in the 1960s through a congressional effort led by Robert Kennedy. It was later disbanded at national level but kept active at state and local level.

It was responsible for investigating and eventually accelerating the downfall of many high-level Mafiosi. It also eliminated much of the organised crime in the Teamsters across the country.

In 1963 Joe Valachi gave the first real insight into the American mafia, as described in the previous chapter.

1969 saw the publication of the bestselling novel "THE GODFATHER" by Mario Puzo. It was made into a film in 1972. As we look back, it is amazing to consider that this book was brought out at a time when Carlo Gambino was operating at the height of the Gambino Family operations. In the meantime, back in Sicily, Luciano Leggio was at his height, with the able support of Riina and Provenzano. The second Mafia war was yet to be unleashed by the men of Corleone.

It is perceived that the Mafia approved of the glamorous aspects of their portrayal in both the book and the film. With the survival of Mario Puzo, this is the only conclusion we can come to!

In 1970 The Racketeer Influenced and Corrupt Organisations Act (RICO Act) was passed. This act made it a crime to belong to an organisation that performed illegal acts, and it created programs such as the witness protection program. Frequent use of the act began during the late 70s and early 80s. Charges of racketeering were successfully pressed against scores of mobsters, including 3 of New York's Godfathers.

In 1976 the FBI achieved a great coup, by having an undercover agent named Joe Pistone infiltrate the Bonanno Family. He posed as a jewel thief under the assumed name of Donnie Brasco. He showed remarkable bravery and played this role for 6 years from 1976 till 1982. He was eventually pulled out when the mob wanted to initiate him, which would have course required him to kill someone. His evidence at The Mafia Commission Trial and The Pizza Connection Trial helped the conviction of some 200 mobsters.

In 1985, many of the top bosses of the Commission were indicted by District Attorney Rudolph Giuliani in what became known as the Mafia Commission Trial. Those to be found guilty included:

- Anthony Corallo--- boss of the Lucchese Family.
- Anthony Salerno--- boss of the Genovese Family.
- Carmine Persico --- boss of the Colombo Family.
- Philip Rastelli --- boss of the Bonnano Family.

In fact the Bonnano Family was still not represented on the Commission because of its previous drug dealing, which was considered by the others to be offensive.

All of them received jail terms of 50-100 years together with very large fines. Gambino Family boss Paul Castellano who had also been indicted was murdered in Times Square before the trial began whereas Dellacroce died of cancer a few months before the trial.

The RICO Act was a valuable instrument for this trial which lasted 34 days and which proved the lethal and vicious control that the Commission exerted over the criminal activities of the Mafia. These activities were proven to pervade almost every area of life in New York. It continues to be used to great effect even today, and has hurt the mob severely. The beheading of the Commission by the use of The Rico Act and the use of high technology was hoped to decimate the Mafia to the point where it may never recover.

This trial was both held and completed in 1986.

1986 saw The Pizza Connection Trial which was the first time that the Sicilian and American Mafia were brought to justice for the large-scale narcotics trafficking which they had inflicted on the United States. This trial was again driven by Rudy Giuliani and was immaculately researched and prepared. The purpose was to prove that a national chain of Mafia owned pizzerias was used to launder huge amounts of drug money, before it found its way to Swiss bank accounts.

The Bonnano Family were very central to this trial because of their heavy commitment to narcotics involvement.

The star witness for the prosecution was Tommaso Buscetta who was described as the biggest canary since Joe Valachi.

A previous chapter relates how Buscetta was deported from South America to Sicily to face previous murder charges.

Because his family had been decimated by the Mafia in the second Mafia war in Sicily, he took revenge by becoming a star pentito at the Maxi Trial which was successfully driven by Judge Falcone.

He then agreed to repeat the performance in New York on the condition that his current wife and their son were given new identities and protection. The court was in raptures at his revelations of life inside the Mafia.

During the trial, one of the defendants, Gaetano Mazzara was brutally murdered. His body was found in a plastic garbage bag in Brooklyn. His legs were broken, his head mutilated, and an attempt had been made to rip his tongue out.

The trial continued and in March 1987, 17 defendants were found guilty and received various lengthy jail sentences of up to 45 years.

Born in Brooklyn where his father had a tavern, Rudy Giuliani was 42 years of age in 1986 when these important cases were being tried. He was an Italian American who deeply resented the damaging reputation given to his ethnic group by the Mafia. He had been encouraged by his father to stand up and make a positive difference in support of Italian Americans.

After 1986, things became much more difficult for the mob. Many of the young American born Mafiosi seemed to lack the disciplines of earlier generations. As a result there was an effort to tighten up the rules of conduct.

The problems for the Mafia included:

- Increasing infiltration by undercover cops.
- Mafiosi turning pentito because of the appeal of the witness protection program. This flew in the face of the tradition of omerta.
- More sophisticated bugging equipment.
- Better quality surveillance equipment.
- The increasing development of information technology.
- The RICO Act.
- The younger generation of Mafiosi becoming less disciplined and more obsessed with celebrity e.g.: John Gotti compared with Sicily's Riina and Provenzano.

There was an attempt to go back to the old methods and style of business, by importing large numbers of Sicilians who were steeped in these traditions. They were known as Zips. They respected the old style methods, had a great "work ethic" and were contemptuous of the sloppiness of the younger American born Mafiosi.

They were usually illegal immigrants, which meant they had no known records or form. By not being on the radar, and by being clean skins, they had an advantage over the agencies of law enforcement.

At this point, the Mafia was down but not out after the onslaught by Giuliani. The question remained as to whether it could regroup, and whether the Zips would take over.

Since the September 11th 2001 Twin Tower attacks, law enforcement agencies became concerned about the resurgence of the Mafia, as it regrouped from its turmoil of the 1990s. This resurgence was made possible because the FBI and other agencies naturally focussed more on homeland security, and away from organised crime.

In 2002, the FBI estimated that the mafia earned $50-90 billion per year. While other criminal organisations such as Russian mobsters, Chinese gangsters, Mexican cartels and others had all grabbed a share of criminal activities, the Mafia continued to be dominant, partly due to its strict hierarchical structure, and partly due to its abilities to adapt and outsource.

In 2006 it was revealed that two decorated detectives had moonlighted as Mafia hit-men. Louis Eppolito (54) and Stephen Caracappa (64) were accused of the bloodiest and most violent betrayal of the police badge that New York had ever seen. They were simultaneously on the payroll of both the city's police force and the Lucchese crime Family. They were working for underboss Anthony Casso and acted as executioners.

They used their police credentials to pull over the cars of victims.

Their crimes included:

- Bruno Facciola was found dead in the boot of a car with a canary stuffed in his mouth after the two officers had fingered him as a federal informant.
- Mobster Jimmy Hydell who was suspected of being the gunman in an attempt to execute Casso, was abducted by the policemen to be tortured and murdered by Casso.
- In one case their information was wrong and an innocent man was killed whilst having Christmas dinner with his mother.
- In the case of Eddie Lino of the Gambino Family, they pulled him over on Brooklyn Bridge, and Caracappa put a bullet in his head (one behind the ear).

Eppolito was the son of a crime family member, and was a small-time actor who had a bit-part in the mob movie Goodfellas.

The pair came under suspicion in 1985, but at the time there was insufficient evidence.

They then retired to luxury homes in Las Vegas, but the smell of corruption lingered in the corridors of America's largest police force.

Their fate was sealed when a jailed mobster turned pentito.

The pair were found guilty of 8 murders and 70 counts of racketeering.

Eppolito's 1992 biography makes fascinating reading, as he paints himself as a hero of policing against the ruthless criminals of New York. He then proceeds to paint himself as a victim of smearing and injustice by the Police Department. He claims he felt broken by their ingratitude and the way that he was shunned!!

Casso is now in jail for 36 murders and according to some sources is said to be losing his mind.

In 2011, the American Mafia cooperates in various criminal activities, including the Sicilian Mafia and other Italian organised crime groups, such as the Camorra, 'Ndrangheta and Sacra Corona Unita, although it no longer operates nationwide.

Law enforcement agencies still consider the Mafia to be the largest organised crime group in the USA.

In 2011, most of the Mafia's activities are contained to the North-eastern United States (New York, Philadelphia, New England, Detroit, and Chicago) where they continue to dominate crime, despite increasing numbers of street gangs and other organisations that are not of Italian origin.

On January 20th 2011, the United States Justice Department issued 16 indictments against northeast American Mafia Families, resulting in 127 people being charged, and more than 110 arrests. The charges included murder, murder conspiracy, loan sharking, arson, robbery, narcotics trafficking, extortion, illegal gambling and labour racketeering.

It has been described as the largest operation against the Mafia in US history.

Families that have been affected include the Five Families of New York as well as the DeCavalcante crime Family of New Jersey, and the Patriarca Family of New England.

One of the arrested was 76 year old Andrew Russo, who is alleged to be head of the Colombo Family and a previous hit man. He was further alleged to have killed a rival in 1993 during the power struggle for control of the Colombo Family.

Surprisingly Hollywood actor, 70 year old James Caan has jumped to his defence and voiced his support. He described him as a wonderful friend and godfather to his son Scott. He then offered to stand bail for Russo.

Caan had played hot tempered Sonny Corleone in the 1972 classic film THE GODFATHER --- further evidence that the Mafia had enjoyed their portrayal.

We can safely assume that Organised crime in America is here to stay. The question remains as to whether the Mafia will continue to be a dominant player, or whether the recent victories by law enforcement will reduce their insidious potency…

POST SCRIPT

There is a considerable amount of newsreel footage available that puts faces to a number of the names mentioned in this American section. These images bring to life the story of the American Mafia.

It never ceases to amaze that the aging Carlo Gambino was the head of such a ruthless criminal organisation. His power was absolute, despite his appearance being so benign.

Glossary of Terms

Associate – an uninitiated man who works for the Mafia.

Capo di tutti capi – boss of all the bosses.

Capo dei capi – boss of bosses.

Capo famiglia (capo) – elected boss of the local gang, clan, cosca or Family.

Capodecina – the boss of a group of about 10 soldiers.

Caporegime – the boss of a group of about 10 soldiers.

Commission – similar to a board of management for the whole mafia.

Consiglieri – adviser to the boss.

Cosa Nostra – our thing a.k.a. the Mafia.

Cosca (Cosche) – a Mafia Family.

Mandamento (Mandamenti) – the district created by 3 Families with adjoining territories.

Omerta – the code of silence.

Pentito (pentiti) – defecting Mafiosi who gives information and evidence against the Mafia.

Pizzo – protection money.

Soldier – the basic rank of a Mafioso.

Sotto capo – the underboss to the capo.